Rope & Faggot

The African American Intellectual Heritage Series

Rope & Faggot

A Biography of Judge Lynch

with A New Introduction
by Kenneth Robert Janken

by
Walter White

UNIVERSITY OF NOTRE DAME PRESS
Notre Dame, Indiana

Library of Congress Cataloging-in-Publication Data
White, Walter Francis, 1893–1955.
    Rope & faggot : a biography of Judge Lynch / by Walter White ;
introduction and bibliography by Kenneth Robert Janken.
        p.   cm. — (African American intellectual heritage series)
    Originally published: New York : Knopf, 1929.
    Includes bibliographical references and index.
    ISBN 0-268-04006-0 (cl. : alk. paper)
    ISBN 0-268-04007-9 (pbk. : alk. paper)
    1. Lynching—United States.   2. African Americans.
3. United States—Race relations.   I. Title: Rope and faggot.
II. Title.   III. Series.

HV6457 .W45   2001
364.1'34—dc21   2001037600

∞ *This book is printed on acid-free paper.*

CONTENTS

ROPE & FAGGOT
by Walter White

INTRODUCTION TO
THE NEW EDITION

Kenneth Robert Janken

In October 1926, Walter White, assistant secretary of
the National Association for the Advancement of Colored People, author of two Harlem Renaissance–era
novels, and courageous investigator of incidents of racial
violence, broke the story of a triple lynching in Aiken,
South Carolina. Bertha, Dedmon, and Clarence Lowman had been taken by more than thirty vigilantes from
the jail where they were being held while on trial on
trumped-up charges of the murder of a deputy sheriff.
They were carried for more than a mile to the lynching spot, where more than one thousand spectators as-
sembled to watch the murders. The assistant secretary's
undercover inquiry exposed rampant official corrup-
tion, lawlessness, and rapid growth of the Ku Klux Klan.
He forwarded to the state's governor, who had publicly
vowed to bring to justice those responsible, a partial list
of mob members, including local law enforcement officials, politicians, prominent businessmen, and two of
the governor's relatives. The governor did nothing.
White turned his findings and contacts over to the *New
York World,* which sent its star reporter to Aiken and ran a
multipart exposé that received national attention. Aiken

was the light-complexioned White's forty-first incognito lynching investigation in eight years; in that time he had also probed eight race riots. He returned to New York relieved to be back above the "Smith and Wesson" line, as he called the Mason-Dixon. He was also drained by the experience and decided to take a leave of absence from the NAACP to pursue writing.

Having written the critically acclaimed *Fire in the Flint* (1924) and then *Flight* (1926), White wanted to try his hand at book-length nonfiction. The assistant secretary applied for and received a year-long Guggenheim Foundation fellowship to move to France and write, among other works, his anti-lynching treatise, *Rope and Faggot*. The grant was to commence in April 1927, but White arranged a later start to allow his wife Gladys time to recuperate from the anticipated birth of their second child (a boy, Walter Carl Darrow, to complement their daughter Jane) in June. On 23 July Walter White, *en famille*, boarded the Cunard line's *Carmania*, bound for Havre. With the $2,500 Guggenheim stipend supplemented by three months paid leave from the association, the Whites settled in Villefranche-sur-Mer in suburban Nice, in a white stone villa on a hill overlooking the Mediterranean. A Bon Marché grocery and Galleries Lafayette department store were twenty minutes away by tram. It was a bargain at the equivalent of fifty American dollars monthly. The Whites remained in Villefranche for six months, but when the tourist season made the Côte d'Azur too expensive, the White ménage relocated to Avignon. Here White felt he could keep in touch with the Anglophone authors—he kept company with Ford Maddox Ford and Somerset Maugham—while sampling a part of France that was not overrun with vacationing Americans and Brits or refugees from Mussolini's Italy. In both places he worked steadily on *Rope and Faggot*.[1]

Subtitled "A Biography of Judge Lynch," *Rope and Faggot* is an outstanding example of partisan scholarship. It is based upon White's firsthand investigations and a sampling of the relevant social scientific literature. The volume fulfilled two interrelated goals: it debunked Southern whites' big lie that lynching punished black men for raping white women and protected the purity of the flower of the white race, and it delivered a penetrating critique of the Southern culture that nourished this blood sport. In the tradition of Ida B. Wells-Barnett at

1. Walter White (WFW) to William Aspinwall Bradley, 20 June 1927, Papers of the NAACP (Bethesda, Md.: University Publications of America, 1993), part 2, reel 11, frame 54, microfilm. Hereinafter cited as NAACP/mf, followed by a part, reel, and frame number; Board of Directors (B of D) Minutes, 14 March 1927, NAACP/mf p1 r2 f134. On life in Villefranche, see WFW to James Weldon Johnson, 16 August 1927, James Weldon Johnson Papers, series 1, folder 539, Beinecke Rare Book and Manuscript Library, Yale University, New Haven, Conn.; WFW to Arthur Spingarn, 16 August 1927, Arthur Spingarn Papers, box 948, folder 175, Moorland-Spingarn Research Center, Howard University, Washington, D.C. (hereinafter cited as Arthur Spingarn Papers/HU); WFW to Bradley, 6 July 1927, NAACP/mf p2 r11 f60; WFW to Johnson, 1 January 1928, NAACP/mf p2 r11 f146. On relocation to Avignon and contact with Anglophone writers, see WFW to Spingarn, 9 January 1928, Arthur Spingarn Papers/HU, box 948, folder 175; WFW to Johnson, 21 February 1928, Johnson papers, series 1, folder 539; WFW to Johnson, 13 October 1927, NAACP/mf p1 r24 f705; WFW to Johnson, 1 January 1928, NAACP/mf p2 r11 f146.

the turn of the twentieth century, White marshaled statistics demonstrating that accusations of rape or attempted rape accounted for less than 30 percent of lynchings. In those cases where the lynch victim did have sexual contact with a white female, White cast doubt on the veracity of the accusers. The assistant secretary identified four categories of girls or women likely to scream "rape": adolescents who were grappling with their nascent sexuality; middle-aged women, who, he implied, were open to sexual experimentation; wives trapped in long-term marriages to "unattractive" men; and "spinsters," who, again, he conjectured, sought some outlet for their sexual expression.[2] Brandishing evidence of white females of all classes crossing the color line for love—evidence that white supremacists themselves broadcast in order to agitate whites to support antimiscegenation laws—White insisted that most interracial liaisons were consensual and not forced.

How to account for the fury and sadism with which the mob attacked lynch victims? Despite the popular notion that whites held darker peoples repugnant and repulsive, white Southern males since the time of slavery had been attracted to black females. Through rape or concubinage, white men had taken advantage of black females, although to justify their aggression they im-

2. Walter White, *Rope and Faggot: A Biography of Judge Lynch* (New York: Knopf, 1929; reprint, Notre Dame, Ind.: University of Notre Dame Press, 2001), 58. Subsequent references will appear in parentheses in the text.

pugned them by claiming that black women were "naturally licentious."[3] The lynchers' savagery, including castration, was born of the unarticulated suspicion that, despite protestations to the contrary, sexual attraction across the color line ran more than one way, and "the absence of repulsion applies to both sexes of both races" (67). Through the act of lynching, the mobbist was projecting his own guilt about his sexual licentiousness on a black scapegoat and also intimidating white women who might find black men attractive (66–68).[4] But, White again emphasized, "the usual crime" was not normally the stimulus for the formation of the mob, although the cry of rape still circulated with alarming frequency because of whites' obsession with sex. At bottom, White asserted, whites employed lynching to keep blacks in their "place" and, more specifically, as a way to control the black labor force (76–77).

As White showed in his chapter "The Economic Foundations of Lynch-Law," lynching first appeared in Virginia in the years immediately preceding the Revolutionary War as a way for Patriots to mete out punishment

3. Jacqueline Jones Royster, introduction to *Southern Horrors and Other Writings: The Anti-Lynching Campaign of Ida B. Wells, 1892–1900* (Boston: Bedford, 1997), 20.

4. For an outstanding discussion of the psychosexual dimensions of lynching, see Trudier Harris, *Exorcizing Blackness: Historical and Literary Lynching and Burning Rituals* (Bloomington, Ind.: Indiana University Press, 1984). See also Donald G. Mathews, "The Southern Rite of Human Sacrifice," *Journal of Southern Religion* (Online) 3 (2000): section three, available at http://jsr.as.wvu.edu/mathews.htm (accessed 29 November 2000).

to Loyalists. With established courts of law more than two hundred miles distant, Thomas Lynch, a local person of considerable influence, established an extralegal tribunal to deal with the Patriots' opponents, who, if convicted, were lashed and made to shout "Long Live Liberty!" A similar method of summary judgment appeared in the western territories as they were being settled by Euro-Americans and before the establishment of a recognized authority. With the invention of the cotton gin and the renewed profitability and expansion of slavery in the early nineteenth century, lynch-law, as it came to be known, became an important measure for the defense of slavery. Beginning around 1830, the planter class employed the rope and faggot with increasing frequency against white and black abolitionists and enslaved Africans suspected of having rebellious intentions. In the decade of the 1850s, what Walter White termed "obviously incomplete" data showed that twenty-six blacks were killed by mobs for "killing their masters" (92).

The South produced one of its most gory chapters during the Reconstruction that followed the Civil War. An 1872 Congressional investigation into Ku Klux Klan violence found that during a span of a few weeks in 1868 more than 2,000 African Americans were murdered by mobs in Louisiana; an incomplete count in Texas revealed that 1,035 were lynched between the end of the Civil War and 1868. Other Southern states posted similarly gruesome statistics. These sanguinary efforts to return African Americans as close to slavery as possible had their effects. As historian Eric Foner noted, the violence, while widespread, was also focused on black politicians, community leaders, and activists; it was largely responsible for the overthrow of Reconstruction state governments and the final end of that experiment in multiracial democracy in 1877.[5] By the end of the century, most of the former Confederacy had disfranchised African Americans and was well on the way to constructing the edifice of legal segregation.

Lynching did not end with the vanquishing of African Americans from public life. Between 1890 and 1930 it was used with a high level of frequency to keep African Americans in their place by policing racial boundaries, punishing and terrorizing prosperous African Americans, and squelching hints of black opposition to the racial order. While many of the twentieth century's spectacular public lynchings involved charges of black males' sexual transgressions, such accusations were not always the proximate cause of mob action; rather, rape was often used as an excuse for a lynching, as a way to enforce a white male consensus. But some of the members of the public mobs, such as the May 1918 murders of Mary Turner and about a dozen others near Valdosta, Georgia, openly avowed their intentions to control black labor. Countless other instances of murder, especially those sparked by labor unrest, were carried out privately, without publicity.[6]

5. Eric Foner, *Reconstruction: America's Unfinished Revolution, 1863–1877* (New York: Harper & Row, 1988), 119–23, 425–44.

6. Walter White, "The Work of a Mob," *The Crisis*, September 1918, 221–23; Grace Elizabeth Hale, *Making Whiteness* (New York: Pantheon, 1998), 201, 202; W. Fitzhugh Brundage, *Lynching in the New South* (Urbana, Ill.: University of Illinois Press, 1993), 62–63, 111–13.

The impulse to lynch was embedded in small town and rural Southern culture and economy, though the impetus appeared, too, in the industrial North. White states that "lynching often takes the place of the merry-go-round, the theatre, the symphony orchestra, and other diversions common to large communities" (9). The absence of cultural institutions like these was a manifestation of the authority of fundamentalist Christianity over life in the South. But, as the historian Grace Hale has shown, while the fundamentalist regime could keep these institutions out of large portions of the South, it could not stop modernity and its attendant culture of consumption, which profoundly affected the lynching industry. Affordable train fares, the diffusion of automobile ownership, a growing telephone network, and the widespread appearance of inexpensive photographs all contributed to the popularization of spectacle violence and its commodification. Notice of an impending lynching could be sent out in advance; participants and observers could organize special railroad excursions or car caravans; photographers could appear and quickly develop souvenir photos for those who wanted to send a postcard to family or friends or who were simply not lucky enough to procure a part of the victim's body. In the twentieth century, lynching became a shared cultural event—either in person or in retelling—that helped to define the identity of white Southerners.[7]

---

7. Hale, *Making Whiteness*, chap. 5.

From colonial times, Christianity, particularly the Southern Baptist and Methodist varieties, absorbed race prejudice into the core of its faith, offering defenses of slavery and refusing to emancipate enslaved Africans who underwent religious conversions (44–45). Southern fundamentalism became, in the words of French social scientist André Siegfried, whom White quoted, "the religion of the Anglo-Saxon or 'superior' race" (44). The convergence of fundamentalist dogma and racist ideology, which supported the plantocracy, produced an overlap of the religious and terrorist leadership that enforced Jim Crow. Preachers populated the Ku Klux Klan hierarchy; even those who were not associated with the Klan gave silent assent to the mob and rarely spoke against it. Lynching was a salient feature of the Protestant Christian dictatorship in the South. Other features included Know-Nothingism and the proliferation of antievolution statutes, which culminated in the 1925 Scopes monkey trial. So long as white Southerners filtered their views on race through the primitive beliefs and assertions of fundamentalism—and so long as the ministry continued to recruit men of at best mediocre intelligence—the assistant secretary saw little hope for the benighted region.

Individual African Americans were not the only ones to pay the price of lynching, White believed; the entire South paid a price as well. The preachers and New South Democratic politicians enforced a rigid conformity in all controversial matters, of which the rope and faggot was an extreme example; but its debilitating effects could

also be found in the extraordinary difficulty white workers faced in organizing labor unions. The Southern
press, when it was not eagerly announcing impending
lynchings, was simply incapable of performing its functions as watchdog and disseminator of critical information. As John Egerton, author of *Speak Now against the
Day* (1994), has shown, a staggering number of Southern
authors, intellectuals, artists, and musicians—African
American and white alike—fled the region's sterile cli-
mate in order to produce their works of culture.

Rope and Faggot builds upon the trailblazing work of
Ida B. Wells-Barnett. A pioneer of the anti-lynching crusade, Wells-Barnett had been active for more than two
decades before White began his work as an NAACP investigator. Her principal writings on lynching offered a
scathing critique of white manliness and white civilization's colossal struggle against black barbarity. It was
Afro-America, she claimed, that expressed manly qualities in its heroic gains in education and living standards.
White men's concupiscence proved them unfit for civilization. They squandered their vital energies raping or
abetting the rape of black women, finally turning their
lust to dominate on black men, who expressed the finer
qualities of civilization.[8]

---

8. Ida B. Wells-Barnett's principal writings on lynching are collected
in *Southern Horrors and Other Writings: The Anti-Lynching Campaign of Ida B.
Wells, 1892–1900*, ed. Jacqueline Jones Royster (Boston: Bedford, 1997).
An insightful analysis of the campaign is found in Gail Bederman, "'Civilization,' the Decline of Middle-Class Manliness, and Ida B. Wells's Anti-
lynching Campaign (1892–94)," *Radical History Review*, no. 52 (1992):
5–30.

That White did not acknowledge or even mention her pathbreaking work can be attributed to both the passage of time and the NAACP's disputes with Wells-Barnett. By the mid-1920s, when White was composing *Rope and Faggot*, Ida Wells-Barnett, who could be difficult to work with, was well past the acme of her lifework and was remembered only dimly, if at all, as a cranky and heroic fighter of the past. This historical indignity was compounded by White's personal—and the NAACP's collective—antagonism toward Wells-Barnett, dating to the association's founding and to divergent opinions about the direction of the anti-lynching crusade.[9]

The NAACP and Wells-Barnett differed on the role of women in the anti-lynching crusade. Because lynching called into question issues of black manhood and male power within the black community, "African American women's initiative against racial violence promoted gender anxiety" according to Patricia Schechter, one of Wells-Barnett's biographers. What African American women could do to stem the epidemic of mobbism was circumscribed by traditional notions of gender and respectability. Ida B. Wells-Barnett's brand of agitation usurped the leadership of the NAACP and other organizations and made them uncomfortable. The NAACP especially was moving away from a model of race advancement through agitation and toward one of institutionalizing the fight for equality by establishing a civil rights bureaucracy. The appropriate type of black

9. On Ida B. Wells and the NAACP, see Paula Giddings, *When and Where I Enter* (New York: William Morrow, 1984), 180–81.

women's anti-lynching work, in the opinion of White and the NAACP, was moral suasion. Though Wells-Barnett also believed in moral suasion, her approach was too confrontational. While the assistant secretary and others frowned upon Wells-Barnett's activism, the association supported and partially bankrolled the work of the "Anti-Lynching Crusaders," a network of black women whose program included fund-raising, education, and building relationships with white Southern women.[10] In order to facilitate this last activity, the Anti-Lynching Crusaders excised from their analysis of mob violence the idea that the interracial sexual contact that was used as an excuse for the murder of black men was in fact consensual; it was this dimension of the lynching epidemic that was at the heart of Wells-Barnett's argument.

Viewed retrospectively, *Rope and Faggot* wears unevenly. The overview of the lynching industry, written in modulated tones, is for that very reason powerful. The

10. Patricia A. Schechter, "Unsettled Business: Ida B. Wells against Lynching, or, How Antilynching Got Its Gender," in *Under Sentence of Death: Lynching in the South*, ed. W. Fitzhugh Brundage (Chapel Hill, N.C.: University of North Carolina Press, 1997), 308, 309. See also Deborah Gray White, "The Cost of Club Work, the Price of Black Feminism," in *Visible Women: New Essays on American Activism*, ed. Nancy A. Hewitt and Suzanne Lebsock (Urbana and Chicago: University of Illinois Press, 1993), 247–69; Dorothy Salem, *To Better Our World: Black Women in Organized Reform, 1890–1920* (Brooklyn, N.Y.: Carlson, 1990), 145–79; and Rosalyn Terborg-Penn, "African-American Women's Networks in the Anti-Lynching Crusade," in *Gender, Class, Race, and Reform in the Progressive Era*, ed. Noralee Frankel and Nancy S. Dye (Lexington, Ky.: University Press of Kentucky, 1991), 148–61. On the Anti-Lynching Crusaders, see B of D Minutes, 11 September 1922, NAACP/mf p1 r1 f903; 13 November 1922, NAACP/mf p1 r1 f913; 11 December 1922, NAACP/mf p1 r1 f917; and 8 January 1923, NAACP/mf p1 r1 f923.

chapter on sex is provocative. The extensive discussion of interracial love and families that acknowledge both their black and white members gave lie to the white supremacists' attempts to use rape as an excuse for lynching and to naturalize racism and segregation. White's discussion of Southern white men's psychosexual anxieties as a cause of lynching still contains much explanatory power. The strongest sections deal with the economic and structural foundations of lynching. Here White identified the maintenance of the plantation economy and its attendant sharecropping and peonage systems as a principal stimulus for mob terror. As to the connection between the two, White wrote, "All of these reasons for the dominance of sex as a factor in lynching, with all their other complications, centre in one objective—economic ascendancy over Negro labour" (76). Stewart E. Tolnay and E. M. Beck, authors of the most ambitious and thorough sociological study of lynching, found that "although we have arrived at our respective destinations by traversing very different terrain, our conclusions overlap significantly with those reached much earlier by White. . . ."[11]

The intervening years since *Rope and Faggot*'s publication have revealed the limitations of White's religious and cultural explanations of the lynching phenomenon. His reflections that the mob was suffused with the fundamentalist Protestant spirit and that its leadership

11. Stewart E. Tolnay and E. M. Beck, *A Festival of Violence: An Analysis of Southern Lynchings, 1882–1930* (Urbana and Chicago: University of Illinois Press, 1995), 255.

often wore clerical garb are suggestive, and his recita-
tion of examples of ritual brutality remains as insightful
as it is horrifying. Yet keen eye for detail notwithstand-
ing, he did not develop these empirical observations
into a thorough critique of the religious and communal
meanings of ritual violence. That task would fall to other
scholars.

With the defeat of the South in the Civil War, "Lost
Cause" mythology developed a strong fundamentalist
foundation. According to sociologist Orlando Patterson,
white Southerners came to believe they lost the war because they were insufficiently righteous or because God
was testing and preparing them for a glory even greater
than the antebellum past. The various symbols and
stages of mob violence—the use of fire and the cross; the
infliction of physical pain on the victim before death; the
preference for lynching sites laden with sacred connotations such as trees and bridges; the popularity of Sunday
for the day of execution—exude religiosity. Lynching,
wrote Patterson, is ritual sacrifice that "enacts and sym-
bolically recreates a disrupted or threatened social
world, and it resolves, through the shedding of blood, a
specific crisis of transition."[12] The popularization of photography and sound recordings made possible vicarious
enjoyment of the event.[13] In other words, white South-

12. Orlando Patterson, *Rituals of Blood: Consequences of Slavery in Two
American Centuries* (Washington, D.C.: Civitas/CounterPoint, 1998), 175.
Chapter 2 is a penetrating study of the Protestant fundamentalist religious dimensions of lynching.
13. Hale, *Making Whiteness*, 227.

erners' communal response to the overthrow of slavery and the social and economic uncertainty created by African Americans' drive for equality was the establishment of the civil religion of the "Lost Cause" and the staging of human sacrifices. But "angry as he was at whites' religion," notes Donald Mathews, a historian of Southern religions, Walter White "did not probe the internal punitiveness of a religion he identified with ignorance and fanaticism to think about the sacred nature of the violence he documented in his work."[14]

H. L. Mencken tried to steer White in this analytical direction when he encouraged him to write for the *American Mercury* about the technique of lynching, but Mencken deemed White's efforts to be "feeble and ineffective." They concentrated, said Mencken, not on the rituals but on lynching's historical contexts, ground White ably covered in *Rope and Faggot*. In both the book and the subsequent article, "The Technique of Lynching," the assistant secretary seemed to content himself with a general exposition of the problem of mob violence flavored with Mencken's distaste, expressed as irony, for Nordic civilization and narrow-minded Protestant fundamentalism.[15]

14. Donald G. Mathews, "The Southern Rite of Human Sacrifice," *Journal of Southern Religion* (Online) 3 (2000): section three, available at http://jsr.as.wvu.edu/mathews.htm (accessed 29 November 2000).

15. H. L. Mencken to WFW, 23 December 1929, and WFW, "The Technique of Lynching," both in NAACP Papers, group II, series L, box 21, "H. L. Mencken 1920–29," Manuscript Division, Library of Congress, Washington, D.C.

While these are not insignificant shortcomings, they do not detract from the book's contemporary and historical significance. *Rope and Faggot* was a powerful indictment of the lynching industry and it garnered excellent reviews. A few publications, perhaps discomfited by the subject matter, found fault with what they thought was overly excitable prose. University of Chicago sociologist Ellsworth Faris in *The New Republic* (8 May 1929) kindly understood that "Mr. White cannot be reasonably expected to be calm." But Leon Whipple at *Survey* (1 October 1929) obtusely made the point that his "controversial bent" led White "to make too much of beating down the straw men of exploded or eccentric doctrines," like pseudo-scientific racism and white males' jealousy of black men's virility (at a time when both ideas enjoyed much currency). However, most praised the author's care in stating his case. *Time* (24 June 1929) hailed White for an "arresting exposition of a not-yet-vanished U.S. folkway." The review incited vicious protests from that magazine's readers. Robert E. Lee of Greenville, North Carolina fulminated that "if anyone needed a coat of tar and feathers it's the author of 'Judge Lynch.'" Eldon Holdane of Atlanta declared that "down here we don't care if all the Negroes are lynched, or even burned or slit open with knives. The outrageous, damnable, unbearable spectacle of lawlessness of the Negro is infinitely greater than would be the entire extermination of the cursed race by the white man." White was delighted by this excoriation. He knew there was no such thing as bad publicity, and he delighted in the wider exposure these denunciations brought.[16] Clarence Darrow emphasized in the *New York Herald Tribune* (21 April 1929) that the facts came not from biased reports but from published accounts in the press near the vicinity of the lynching. Melville Herskovits generously praised the book in *The Nation* (15 May 1929) for its "much considered presentation of the highest order" and its "healthy, sane, and desirable" point of view. *Modern Quarterly* editor V. F. Calverton told readers of the *New York World* (28 April 1929) that "in every way it is a challenge to our civilization."

Rope and Faggot endures because of that challenge. Its unvarnished analysis of the causes of lynching was clearer and more uncompromising than most of the sympathetic declarations by the assistant secretary's white contemporaries. Even Arthur Raper's exhaustive *Tragedy of Lynching* (1933), usually identified as the starting point for recent histories of lynching, assigned blacks some culpability for lynching. Contrary to information presented by White, and Wells-Barnett before him, that mobs often singled out successful blacks for retribution, Raper believed that African Americans could do much to stamp out lynching by "demonstrating the ability, character, and good citizenship of the race" and by cooperating with "officials and influential white friends"[17]—favorite nostrums of Booker T. Washington.

16. Letters to the editor, *Time,* 8 July 1929; WFW to Aaron Bernd, 6 July 1929, NAACP/mf p2 r12 f101.
17. Arthur Raper, *The Tragedy of Lynching* (Chapel Hill: University of North Carolina Press, 1933), 38.

Will Alexander, head of the Commission for Interracial Cooperation and one of the most enlightened white Southerners, refused to support the NAACP-backed federal Costigan-Wagner antilynching law; other Southern white liberals, including prominent newspaper editors George Fort Milton and Virginius Dabney, likewise took Alexander's lead in opposing both lynching and the preferred legal remedy to the problem so far as African Americans were concerned.[18]

Rope and Faggot retains its significance, too, because it represents the perspective of African Americans in the fight against mob justice. White insisted on African Americans' humanity, equality, and potential. Neither the book nor its author shrank in the face of hostile white public opinion or shaded a conclusion to gain that public's acceptance. In presenting the harsh truth about lynching, Walter White showed himself to be a passionate, consistent, and articulate pursuer of racial justice.

18. Will Alexander to WFW, 8 April 1935, NAACP/mf p7B r8 f51; George Fort Milton to WFW, 31 January 1935, NAACP/mf p7B r7 f381; Virginius Dabney to WFW, 2 January 1935, NAACP/mf p7B r6 f1226.

Suggested Reading

In addition to the sources cited in the "Introduction to the New Edition," interested readers may consult the following works. The National Association for the Advancement of Colored People kept records of lynchings. *Thirty Years of Lynching in the United States, 1889–1918* (New York: National Association for the Advancement of Colored People, 1919) and the *NAACP Annual Report* for various years contain the grim statistics and circumstances surrounding the mobs' actions. Additionally, *The Crisis*, the organ of the NAACP, regularly carried investigative articles about lynchings. A visual record of the lynching epidemic is contained in *Without Sanctuary: Lynching Photography in America*, ed. James Allen (Santa Fe, N.M.: Twin Palms, 2000). Walter White's first novel, *Fire in the Flint* (New York: Knopf, 1924), deals with lynching; it is one of the works treated in Trudier Harris, *Exorcising Blackness: Historical and Literary Lynching and Burning Rituals* (Bloomington, Ind.: Indiana University Press, 1984). The campaign to extirpate mob violence is chronicled in two outstanding works. Robert L. Zangrando, *The NAACP Crusade against Lynching, 1909–1950* (Philadelphia: Temple University Press, 1980) is a masterful exposition of the association's legislative lobbying and political mobilization. Jacquelyn Dowd Hall, *Revolt against Chivalry*, rev. ed. (New York: Columbia University Press, 1993) concerns the life of the Southern white antilynching crusader Jessie Daniel Ames and reveals both the strong stand that many Southern white females took and the limitations of that region's racial liberalism.

KENNETH ROBERT JANKEN is Associate Professor of Afro-American Studies at the University of North Carolina at Chapel Hill and author of *Rayford W. Logan and the Dilemma of the African-American Intellectual.*

ROPE AND FAGGOT

BY
WALTER WHITE

THE FIRE
IN THE FLINT
1924

FLIGHT
1926

THE LAW IS TOO SLOW
From a lithograph by
George W. Bellows

ROPE & FAGGOT

A BIOGRAPHY OF JUDGE LYNCH

BY

WALTER WHITE

1 9 2 9

ALFRED · A · KNOPF

NEW YORK & LONDON

PREFACE

Twenty-three years ago the late William Graham Sumner of Yale University wrote of lynching: "It would be a disgrace to us if amongst us men should burn a rattlesnake or a mad dog. The badness of the victim is not an element in the case at all. Torture and burning are forbidden, not because the victim is not bad enough, but because we are too good. . . . It is evident, however, that public opinion is not educated up to this level."

More than two decades after Sumner wrote these words, public opinion on burnings and lynchings is not yet educated up to the level where such barbarities are impossible. The number of victims each year has sharply decreased, but the savagery with which the smaller number of victims are tortured by American mobs is proportionately greater than at the turn of the century. From the days when one John Malcolm was "genteely Tarr'd and Feather'd" at Pownalborough, Massachu-

*setts, in 1773, mobbism has inevitably degenerated to
the point where an uncomfortably large percentage of
American citizens can read in their newspapers of the
slow roasting alive of a human being in Mississippi and
turn, promptly and with little thought, to the comic strip
or sporting page. Thus has lynching become an almost
integral part of our national folkways.*

*The present inquiry was begun with the intention of
treating lynching as an isolated phenomenon, but that
idea was of necessity abandoned before the inquiry
had proceeded very far. The reason for this change is
that the deeper one inquires into the subject, the more
one must regard lynching as being of only minor importance in itself; it is as a symptom of a malo-
dorous economic and social condition that it is chiefly
significant. Only such facts are included in the present
study regarding the number, place, and method of lynchings as were deemed necessary for the enlightenment of
those who know little of the situation. From these an effort has been made to isolate and examine the various
ingredients of lynching—economic forces, race prejudice, religion, sex, politics, journalism, and theories of*

racial superiority and inferiority based upon faulty or insufficient scientific evidence.

Haste is made to disavow any pretension that the whole subject is here exhausted. I have attempted to sketch broadly what lies behind the lynching mob and to stimulate thought and discussion upon the subject. There doubtless will be disagreement with some of the conclusions. Such differences will be as valuable as they are inevitable if, out of the discussion which this volume may perhaps arouse, there comes a greater willingness to face more honestly and fully what is one of the most serious problems that faces the United States today.

One of the persons who have read the manuscript of this book has questioned the chapter on the influence of theories of racial superiority and inferiority. The point is made that the brain-weights theory has long since been repudiated by the best students and thus does not merit lengthy consideration. Such a criticism would be valid were this volume designed solely for those whose minds are scientifically trained. Unfortunately, however, the number of those who are not trained so far exceeds that of those who are, that I have thought it necessary to help further to destroy the myth that great or little brain-weight is of any ascertainable value. Superstitions and untruths—especially those which confirm prejudices—die hard. It has been my own experience to encounter in all parts of America a very great number of persons who believe that the Negro brain is much lighter than the white and that ergo the Negro is inferior. Being inferior, crimes against him and impositions upon him are of less moment than similar offences against a white person. "Just another nigger lynched!" all too often is the sole obituary of the latest of Judge Lynch's victims.

No study of lynching, however casual, can fail to reveal the fact that the refusal to discuss certain phases of the question has prevented, more than any other single factor, a possible solution to the problem. Most of the commentators, in fact, have expended a large part of their energy in avoiding those aspects of the subject which might arouse the ill temper or animosity of lynchers and their adherents. Such tender regard for the feelings of lynchers has been abandoned in the present inquiry. I have tried to discuss the problem

*in as temperate and unbiased a manner as possible,
but to write about lynching without discussing religion
and sex among its causes is to leave the root of the
matter unexplained.*

*To many who have been of great help to me I wish
here to make grateful acknowledgment. These, among
many others, include James Weldon Johnson, Arthur
B. Spingarn, and Charles S. Johnson for critical reading
of the entire manuscript; Dr. Raymond Pearl, of Johns
Hopkins University, for much valuable aid and for
reading the chapter on "Science, Nordicism, and Lynching"; Sir Arthur Keith, president of the British Association for the Advancement of Science, for many
useful suggestions in the gathering and use of material
in the same chapter; Miss Beatrice Blackwood, of the
Department of Human Anatomy of Oxford University,
who so patiently aided in the search for authoritative
opinion upon certain questions of the relation between
ability and brain-structure, brain-weight, and head-form;
Dr. W. E. B. DuBois, editor of the* Crisis, *and Dr.
Melville J. Herskovits, of Northwestern University, for
advice, information, and guidance; Professor Robert*

*Bennett Bean, of the University of Virginia, for supply-
ing reprints of certain articles written by him and now
out of print, which were indispensable despite the extent
of my disagreement with certain of Professor Bean's
conclusions; the John Simon Guggenheim Memorial
Foundation and its secretary, Dr. Henry Allen Moe,
through whose generous grant of a fellowship I was
enabled to make this study; the Board of Directors
of the National Association for the Advancement of
Colored People for leave of absence and other aid
in accepting that fellowship; Dr. Will W. Alexander
for information concerning the Interracial Commission
and the movements towards liberalism in the South; and
many others, as well, who have aided, including some
in the South who have supplied information, but whose
names it would be unwise to publish. I wish likewise
to acknowledge my gratitude to many lynchers with
whom I have talked and who have expressed themselves
freely, unaware of my racial identity.*

*Finally, I wish to extend to my wife my thanks for
aid in the selection and arrangement of material and*

for the clarification of ideas through discussions with her. Readers of the book will hardly need to be informed that none of these are responsible for the choice or arrangement of material, or for the conclusions drawn.

W. W.

New York, May 1927 —
Avignon, April 1928

CONTENTS

===

ROPE AND FAGGOT

CHAPTER ONE

THE MIND OF THE LYNCHER

=======

I N FLORIDA some years ago several lynchings and the
burning of the Negro section of the town followed the
attempt of a Negro pharmacist to vote in a national
election. One morning shortly afterwards I walked along
the road which led from the beautiful little town to the
spot where five Negroes had been burned. Three shining-
eyed, healthy, cleanly children, headed for school, approached me. As I neared them, the eldest, a ruddy-
cheeked girl of nine or ten, asked if I was going to the
place where "the niggers" had been killed. I told her I
might stop and see the spot. Animatedly, almost as
joyously as though the memory were of Christmas
morning or the circus, she told me, her slightly younger
companions interjecting a word here and there or nod-
ding vigorous assent, of "the fun we had burning the
niggers."

One need not be a sentimentalist to feel that such
warping of the minds of Southern children is by far
the worst aspect of lynching. All parents appreciate the
difficulty of avoiding in home and in school the inculcation of tendencies towards falsehood, deception, and
dishonesty in the minds of their children. A careless

word of approbation or reproof may find root in the
mind of a child, wholly without the knowledge or intent
of mother or father or teacher, and bear unwholesome
fruit many years later. Psychologists have established
that from birth the human mind passes through all
racial experience—from savagery through barbarism
and upwards to what we term civilization precisely as
the human body from conception to birth passes through
the reptile, fish, and animal stages.

Imagine, then, the mind of a normal child in a Southern community. Its parents throw about him all the protection and give to him all the guidance and tender care
which parents are accustomed to give. A crime is committed or it is alleged that one has been committed.
In law-abiding communities it is bad enough to have
the crime and the trial of the accused discussed in homes
and in the press, worse if there is added the effect of an
execution. But in a community where a lynching or
perhaps a burning occurs, where thousands of participants and spectators include mothers and children of
tender age among them, where there is morbid scram-
bling for charred bones or links of the chain which held
the victim to his funeral pyre, where leaders of the
mob are exalted as men of courage and action—the
effect upon young minds is almost too appalling to be
contemplated. It is entirely within the range of possibilities that such experiences may result in arrestation.
In the unconscious of these immature minds are thus

sown the seeds of lynching as a panacea which will correct all ills and especially those emanating from Negro sources. Primitive impulses to vengeance of violent character upon those whom the possessors of such minds do not like are thus nourished and form one step to further mob murder. Lynchings justified and extolled, lynchers exalted as men of bravery and forthrightness, efforts at punishment of the lynchers blocked and derided—such frequently repeated acts cannot fail to shape young minds in moulds which seem destined later to demand more victims.

Nearly a century of lynching and nearly five thousand mob murders within less than half a century have done an incalculable harm to American minds and particularly in those states where lynchings have been most frequent. Some of the effect can be seen in the frequency with which the phrase is heard—often from the lips of normal, law-abiding people even in the North and West—"he ought to be strung up to a tree."

Pavlov, the Russian psychologist, found that each succeeding generation of the rats he was observing went with fewer lessons at the sound of a bell to a fixed feeding place. Culturally, something of the same reaction to the use of mobbism affects certain Americans as, genetically, affected Pavlov's rats. Approximately similar conditioned responses actuate the human beings and the animals—the bell acted as an excitant for the latter; for the former a crime, real or fancied, by a Negro against a white person served and yet serves as a stimulus to lynching.

Generation after generation of Southern whites have been handicapped and stunted in their mental and moral growth by such a situation. They have had it constantly dinned into their ears from pulpit and press, in the home and school and on the street, that Negroes are given to sex crimes, that only lynching can protect white women, that unmentionably horrible deeds can be prevented only through the use of extreme brutality. Added to this is the belief that any white man, no matter how inept, criminal, or depraved, is infinitely superior to the "best Negro who ever lived." It is a well-known fact that any idea, no matter how unsound, if repeated often enough and in a sufficiently assured manner, is eventually adopted by the mob as its own. One can estimate the long and difficult climb the Southern white child, living in an atmosphere where dissenting opinion is ruthlessly suppressed, must make to attain even a reasonably intelligent attitude towards lynching and the Negro.

William Graham Sumner in his *Folkways* described succinctly the brutalizing effect which lynchings and burnings have had:

"It is an unseemly thing and unworthy of our age and civilization that persons should be lynched for alleged crime without the trial and proof which our institutions provide for. The arguments in defense of lynching (except on the frontier, where civil institutions do not yet exist) never touch on this point. It is unseemly that any one should be burned at the stake in a modern civilized state. It is nothing to the purpose to show what a wicked wretch the victim was. Burning alive has long been thrown out of the folkways of our ancestors. The objection to reviving it is not an apology for the bad men or a denial of their wickedness; it is the goodness of the lynchers. They fall below what they owe to themselves. Torture has long been thrown out of our folkways. It might have been believed a few years ago that torture could not be employed under the jurisdiction of the United States, and that, if it was employed, there would be a unanimous outburst of indignant reprobation against those who had so disgraced us. When torture was employed in the Philippines no such outburst occurred. The facts and the judgment upon them were easily suppressed."

Even though there be some who feel that Sumner was over-optimistic in his certainty that torture had been wholly abandoned, one can agree readily with his picture of the self-inflicted injury to the lyncher. With the exception of the larger centres, and even in some of those, there exists in practically the entire South the possibility of a lynching at any time as a result of generation after generation of mob violence. Here are to be found the most depressing examples of the crowd as defined by Professor Ross, of the University of Wisconsin—"essentially atavistic and sterile . . . the lowest form of human associations." Reaction, ignorance, unrestrained passions, resistance to progress, wild beast joy in causing pain, disease, poverty—these are but a few of the items which lynching has caused to those who practised them. The description of the effect of slavery which Winwood Reade used in *The Martyrdom of Man* applies with equal force to the effect of oppression as represented by mob-law—"the Fathers of the country ate sour grapes, and the children's teeth were set on edge."

Certain factors which have been largely contributory to the low mental estate of the parts of the country where lynching has flourished are treated in later chapters. These include the influence of evangelical religions, the use by unscrupulous politicians of mythical fear of "Negro domination," the important role of sex, and the strenuous efforts to keep the Negro ignorant and intimidated that he may the more easily be exploited. The present chapter is devoted to an attempt to point out some of the factors which have created and are perpetuating the psychology of the lyncher, actual or potential.

Obviously, the lynching states have suffered most from derelict officials. Until very recent times, and in most of the South, even today, no lyncher has ever needed to feel the slightest apprehension regarding punishment or even the annoyance of an investigation. Even in the few instances where there were arrests and trials, the accused usually had friends on the jury, if not fellow lynchers; in others he knew that jurors and court officials were in sympathy with him or else dared not press the case too vigorously.

Some years ago I reported for a New York newspaper a trial in Alabama of a number of men charged with the lynching of two Negroes. Several court officials freely admitted the guilt of the defendants, but accurately foretold early acquittals. "Nobody around here is ever going to vote for convicting a white man for killing a nigger," one of them told me. "Why go to the expense, then, of holding a trial?" I asked, and received the reply: "What with all the talk up North about lynching, we've got to make some show—we're expecting a lot of money to be invested in business down here when they finish the Muscle Shoals dam."

A second ingredient in lynching-psychology is the human love of excitement. Sinclair Lewis and countless of his imitators have painted in leaden colours the Gopher Prairies of the West, but most of these towns are highly diverting when compared with the average small town in the South. The endless routine of drab working-hours and more drab home life, dominated by a relentlessly vitriolic and ignorant ministry, has little of excitement in it. There is much more than levity in the statement of H. L. Mencken that lynching often takes the place of the merry-go-round, the theatre, the symphony orchestra, and other diversions common to large communities. It is not at all unlikely that, whatever their other shortcomings, the radio and the cheap motor car have been and will be not inconsiderable factors in diverting attention from the Negro and in lessening the use of the rope and the torch.

Third among the factors in lynch-law is the human unwillingness to form new ideas, no matter how much evidence is offered regarding the soundness of the new ideas or the falsity of the old. Its general backwardness makes the rural South more susceptible to this malady than any other part of the country. The average Southerner boasts that no one else "knows" the Negro as he does. Yet there are few white people in the South who on hearing the word "Negro" can avoid thinking of but one of three types—or a combination of them. One of these is the happy-go-lucky, improvident, shiftless Negro; the second, a habitual criminal of unrestrained appetites, kept within bounds only by extreme brutality; the third is a humble, "befo' de wah" type, who knows "how to stay in his place." Towards these there are a variety of attitudes, ranging all the way from affection or amused superiority to loathing and extreme fear. Negroes who do not fit snugly and instantly into this limited number of pigeon-holes simply are beyond the comprehension of the average Southern white and they invariably excite resentment or are dismissed as being "unusual" and therefore not worthy of classification. Tenaciously do these older stereotypes cling to life. Continuously do they furnish material for writers of the Octavus Roy Cohen and Irvin Cobb brand of humour.

They serve as insulation to understanding of the Negro and his aims, perpetuate stereotyped thinking and utterances on the most perplexing of American problems, and lead to closed minds, with violence all too often the answer to even the most temperate statements of obvious truths.

But these are the more evident aspects of the lyncher's mind. There are others more subtle and more dangerous. It is little realized that lynching is much more an expression of Southern fear of Negro progress than of Negro crime. No sane man would doubt for a moment that there would be far less lynching if all Negroes could neatly be pigeon-holed into one of the three classifications mentioned, as a buffoon, a criminal, or a menial. One of the most active stimulants of race hatred is the advance—particularly economic—which the Negro has made during the years since the Civil War. There are, of course, many whites in the South who are glad to see this progress, but, unfortunately for the South and for the Negro, there are many whites who bitterly resent his emergence as an individual or as a group from the lowest economic, educational, and cultural position. To quote Mr. Mencken again: "Ku Kluxry is the Southern poor white's answer to the progress of the emerging Negro, once his equal and now threatening to become his superior."

It is not difficult to imagine the inner thoughts of the poor white as he sees members of a race he has been taught by tradition, and by practically every force of public opinion with which he comes into contact, to believe inferior making progress greater than his own. Here, for example, we have a group of poverty-burdened cotton-mill workers or equally poor farmers. In the same town lives a Negro doctor or business man or farmer with a comfortable home, an automobile, a bank account, a radio of the latest model, and well-dressed wife and children. The poor white lives in a shabby house, he has a difficult time in paying for a most meagre living, his wife and children are poorly clad. Physical violence upon the person of the member of the "inferior" race who has dared prove himself not so inferior is the sole balm for the poor white's wounded self-esteem. Out of no more startling circumstances than these have arisen lynchings, not necessarily against the prosperous Negroes, though against them often enough, particularly since the revival of the Ku Klux Klan. That resentment has motivated many men to join a lynching mob. The tendency to direct mob violence against successful Negroes has been especially noticeable during the past ten years of lynching.

There is, however, an even more potent reason for the resort to physical violence in the South. This factor has not often been considered, but upon reflection it will perhaps explain in part, not only lynching mobs, but the general truculence and belligerency of the South. Briefly, it is that the South, from the very beginning of the Negro problem, has been on the defensive and has been defending an indefensible position. Even while the Constitution was being framed, the representatives of Southern planters waged a bitter fight for the retention of slavery, though Jefferson and Madison and Paine saw the inescapable dangers of temporizing with the evil. From the adoption of the Constitution to the Civil War the energy of Southern leaders, headed by the brilliant Calhoun, was almost solely devoted to the losing battle for the maintenance of human bondage. The Bible was frequently called upon in defence of the system, Abraham's ownership of slaves, and the proscription of covetousness toward a neighbour's manservant or maidservant, his ox or his ass, being cited as approval from Heaven of slavery. Press, pulpit, the schoolroom, and every organ of public opinion were made servile and contributory to retention of the system, which was economically unsound, morally indefensible, at odds with the spirit of the age and of the country, and certain to do irremediable harm to those who profited most from it. Yet the more the tide turned against slavery, the more the articulate South defended it.

Charles and Mary Beard in *The Rise of American Civilization* give an interesting picture of this energetic defence by the planting South:

In the long history of defense mechanisms, there is no chapter more fascinating than that which recounts the rise and growth of the extraordinary system of ethics which, at the

very height of the slave power, formed the moral bulwark of
its established order. The system did not, of course, spring
full blown from the mind of any single thinker. It was the
work of many minds, separate departments being added from
year to year under the stress of attack from without and the
pressure of fusion within. At length it was finished—an exhaustive compendium of historical, legal, constitutional, economic, religious, ethical, and philosophical arguments in support of slavery, a vast and intricate body of logic suffused with
the glow of righteous sincerity and adorned with gems of
classical eloquence—a ready and inspiring guide capable of
sustaining those troubled by doubts and fortifying combatants
on the firing line of politics. Representatives in Congress,
newspaper editors in their sanctums, clergymen in their pul-
pits, professors in their institutions of learning, and political
leaders ranging from national figures down to village politicians now had at their tongue's tips a reply to every attack, a foil for every thrust. By the irony of fate the great argument reached its perfection at the very moment when the
economic class for which it provided moral assurance had
passed the peak of its power and, unknown to its defenders,
was tottering on the brink of doom.

Winwood Reade in *The Martyrdom of Man* characterizes the South's attitude of defence in these words:

The Southerners were invariably provincial in their feelings; they did not consider themselves as belonging to a
nation, but a league; they inherited the sentiments of aver-
sion and distrust with which their fathers had entered the
Union; threats and provisoes were always on their lips. . . .
The history of the South within the Union is that of a people
struggling for existence by means of political devices against
the spirit of the nation and the spirit of the age.

Later we shall see how the slave states met the failure of their verbal defence of slavery with lynching,
defended by charges of sex crimes. To understand the
psychology back of this answer of force where logic and
ethics failed, one needs only to consider a familiar
superstition—the notion that all red-headed people are
possessed of fiery tempers and are always ready to engage in physical combat. Neither biologists nor anyone
else has found in the physical or mental constitution
of red-headed human beings any substances which make
them invariably different in temper and combativeness
from those of more ordinary hair-colour; but psychologists have rightly assumed that the temper and the pug-
nacity are a defence mechanism against such derogatory
appellations as "carrot—"or "brick-top." The assertive-
ness, the refusal to listen to arguments opposed to their
own beliefs, the pugnaciousness of Southern congressmen, the indulgence in lynching and other forms of
mob violence and intolerance spring beyond all doubt
in large measure from the same sort of emotions.

The Civil War and the emancipation of the slaves
increased rather than diminished the need for such defence. Defeated both in logic and in the test of armed
strength the South obviously could not find sufficient
solace in sentimental moping over "the lost cause."
Despite preoccupation with expansion and the gathering of wealth, there was a large body of Northern opinion which severely criticized the South's bloody Recon-

struction Period, its lynching, its refusal to accept the
verdict of Appomattox. The Ku Klux Klan, both of the
seventies and of recent years, is a concrete example of
the working of the defence mechanism in its resort to
physical violence. Aware that all peaceful efforts to suppress the Negro are proving increasingly unsuccessful,
the lyncher hopes by increased savagery to achieve the
desired goal. It is this attitude which creates what Frank
Tannenbaum in *Darker Phases of the South* terms "the
South's emotional fixation on the Negro." Having created the mental picture of the Negro as inferior, dangerously addicted to sex crimes, and likely to burst into
unbelievably horrible activities if pressure upon him is
slackened in the least, the South has become the quailed
victim of its own selfishly created fear, which is rooted
in this defence mechanism. The result clearly has
worked for the almost complete closing of many Southern minds to facts or reason. One can argue until one
is blue in the face that the figures do not substantiate
the charge that most lynchings are for protection of
white women; that even if they were, lynching has
been ineffective, as the percentage of lynchings for alleged rape has remained practically constant throughout the past half-century; that white women of the
South have vigorously repudiated lynching as necessary for their protection; that lynching, among its other
faults, has brutalized the lyncher and probably added
to cases where rape or attempted rape actually oc-

curred, by spreading widely stories of such cases and stirring abnormal persons to attempt the same thing. One can do all this, but for a depressingly high percentage of Southern whites, and even of those who are not Southern, the efforts will be fruitless. Too tightly have their minds been bound by the old prejudices and crowd-mindedness.

In his excellent *The Behavior of Crowds* Everett Dean Martin points out that only through liberation from prejudices can come release from crowd-mindedness. Lynching, disfranchisement, "Jim Crow" cars, disgraceful school facilities for Negroes, blindly bitter press and pulpit, court injustice, and a multitude of other methods of keeping the Negro "in his place" have done incalculable harm to the white South in more rigidly fastening upon it a moral, spiritual, and intellectual sterility and blindness. In creating a psychology of oppression of the Negro it has hamstrung itself. Not for the salvation of the Negro, but for its own sake must the South break away from its deadening mental inertia, acquire a vigorous intellectual curiosity which will smash or at least crack the shell of its crowd-mindedness. Fortunately for the white South, for the Negro, and for the United States, there are signs at the University of North Carolina, to a lesser degree at other educational centres, and here and there among individuals, of this new intellectual curiosity, which may save even the most hopelessly backward of the Southern communities. It

seems to be a race between light and darkness, a battle between prejudice and intelligence, to see whether the
lyncher, the opponent of enlightenment, and the narrow-
minded sectionalist can resist the forces from without
and from within which may break up the older thought-
patterns and save the South from itself. Lynching is
but one of the symptoms of intellectual and moral decay resulting from the closed mind which the South
has assumed on many subjects. There is found the apoth-
eosis—and the virus colours most of American thought
on the race question—of James Harvey Robinson's
characterization that " . . . most of our so-called reasoning consists in finding arguments for going on believing as we already do." Judge Lynch's absolutism will
end completely only when open minds and scientific
and health-giving scepticism replace not only the South's
but America's and the white world's present attitude
of snobbism, bigotry, and greed on the questions of
colour and race.

CHAPTER TWO

THE EXTENT OF THE INDUSTRY

A STUDY of the figures of lynchings reveals immediately two contradictory facts. The first of these is encouraging—the rather steady decrease by decades of the total number of victims of Judge Lynch. From 1890 to 1900 there were 1665 persons lynched; from 1900 to 1910 there were 921; from 1910 to 1920 there were 840; and since 1920 through 1927 there were 304. The averages, therefore, for the four divisions of time, successively, are thus 166.5, 92.1, 84.0, and 38.0.

Against this gratifying decrease in number of victims is the greatly aggravated brutality, often extending to almost unbelievable torture of the victim, which has marked lynchings within recent years. This may be attributed partly to the effect of the war—the lust for blood and cruelty which the war did not wholly satiate doubtless stimulated the increase of burnings, mutilations, and other forms of mob sadism. On the other hand, it is entirely safe to assume that had not the war occurred, there would have been some increase in torture in lynching. Indications of this were seen long before the war in Europe began or was seriously thought possible. It came as the inevitable result of many years of lynching—the search of the mob for new thrills when relatively painless hanging or shooting no longer sufficed to appease it. As the user of drugs demands increasing quantities of the opiate upon which he relies for excitation, so does the lyncher demand savagery —always the story of physical cruelty in its effect upon those who practise it.

These harsher methods were seldom practised until the new century had begun. Isolated burnings at the stake, it is true, were known as far back as 1835, but these were so unusual that they created nation-wide discussion and indignation when they occurred. The public conscience had not then become inured to such things. In the *Forum* Walter Hines Page accurately foretold and warned of the danger to the South of unchecked lynching when, in 1893, he said that "the great danger is not in the first violation of the law, nor in the crime itself, but in the danger that Southern public sentiment under the stress of this phase of the race problem will lose the true perspective of civilization."

How true this has been, not only for the South, but for all of the United States, can be seen by examination of the history of lynching during recent years, remembering at the same time the almost unbroken calm with which such conditions have been accepted by all save a few. In the ten years from January 1, 1918, through 1927, American mobs lynched 454 persons. Of these, 38 were white, and 416 were coloured. Eleven of the

Negro victims were women, three of them at the time of lynching with child.

Forty-two of the victims were burned alive. The bodies of sixteen others were burned after death. Eight of the victims were beaten to death or cut to pieces. Sixty-six of 454 lynchings, therefore, were executed with a bestiality unknown even in the most remote and uncivilized parts of the world. Of the sixty-six cases—instances of drowning or of tying the body to an automobile and dragging it through the streets are not included —four were of white victims, three burnings and one beating to death. The remaining sixty-two victims were Negroes. Thus of 416 Negroes lynched within the past ten years sixty-two, or 14.9 per cent—a little less than one out of each seven—were done to death with abnormal savagery. Four of thirty-eight white victims, or 10.5 per cent, suffered the same fate.

The states in which these exhibitions of sadism have occurred are given below in the numerical order of such events.

State	Burnings	Bodies Burned After Death	Beatings or Cuttings to Death	Total
Texas	11	3	2	16
Georgia	8	4	1	13
Florida	8	–	–	8
Mississippi	8	–	–	8
Arkansas	3	2	–	5
Louisiana	1	2	1	4
Alabama	1	–	2	3
Tennessee	1	1	–	2

State	Burnings	Bodies Burned After Death	Beatings or Cuttings to Death	Total
Montana	1	–	–	1
Nebraska	1	–	–	1
California	–	–	1	1
Illinois	–	–	1	1
Kentucky	–	1	–	1
South Carolina	–	1	–	1
Virginia	–	1	–	1
				66

As would be expected, the same states which lead in number of lynchings occupy front rank in brutality of execution. Texas mobs lynched fifty-five persons during these ten years; sixteen, or 29.0 per cent, with sadistic cruelty. Of thirty-four victims Arkansas mobs put five of them to death with similar abnormal viciousness; Florida abused eight of the fifty-six lynched in that state; Mississippi burned alive eight of her sixty-nine victims; thirteen of Georgia's eighty-four victims were lynched otherwise than by the conventional hanging or shooting.

Figures alone could not possibly tell the entire story, however. Let us consider a few authentic and thoroughly corroborated instances of the present-day methods of American mobs. Some of the stories are taken from reliable newspapers, frequently from journals published in the state where the events occurred. These obviously can be relied upon not to overstate the facts. In others the facts are from the reports of competent investigators; in a number from officials of the states in which the lynchings occurred.

Arkansas

Henry Lowry, a Negro of Nodena, had been held in virtual peonage for more than two years by a white landowner. When Lowry, on Christmas Day, 1920, demanded payment of wages due him, he was cursed and struck by the landlord and shot by the landlord's son. Lowry thereupon drew his own gun and killed the landlord and his daughter, who stood near him. Escaping to Texas, he was arrested. The Governor of Arkansas assured him protection from mob violence and a fair trial; so Lowry waived whatever rights he possessed involving interstate rendition. The two Arkansas officers sent to bring him back from Texas ignored the Governor's orders to take Lowry by the shortest route to Little Rock for safe keeping and took him by way of New Orleans and Mississippi. At Sardis, Mississippi, a mob, waiting and obviously advised of the route, "overpowered" the officers. Lowry in their possession, word was sent to other members of the mob who were dining comfortably at the fashionable Peabody Hotel at Memphis. The newspapers were advised in time to issue early afternoon "extras" giving full details as to time, place, and other arrangements for the forthcoming lynching.

Ralph Roddy, a reporter for the Memphis *Press*, a daily newspaper, was sent to cover the event. His story, appearing in the *Press* of January 27, 1921, bore the head: "KILL NEGRO BY INCHES." Here is what Roddy saw and wrote:

. . . More than 500 persons stood by and looked on while the Negro was slowly burned to a crisp. A few women were scattered among the crowd of Arkansas planters, who directed the grewsome work of avenging the death of O. T. Craig and his daughter, Mrs. C. P. Williamson.

Not once did the slayer beg for mercy despite the fact that he suffered one of the most horrible deaths imaginable. With the Negro chained to a log, members of the mob placed a small pile of leaves around his feet. Gasoline was then poured on the leaves, and the carrying out of the death sentence was under way.

Inch by inch the Negro was fairly cooked to death. Every few minutes fresh leaves were tossed on the funeral pyre until the blaze had passed the Negro's waist. . . . Even after the flesh had dropped away from his legs and the flames were leaping toward his face, Lowry retained consciousness. Not once did he whimper or beg for mercy. Once or twice he attempted to pick up the hot ashes in his hands and thrust them in his mouth in order to hasten death.

Each time the ashes were kicked out of his reach by a member of the mob. . . .

As the flames were eating away his abdomen, a member of the mob stepped forward and saturated the body with gasoline. It was then only a few minutes until the Negro had been reduced to ashes. . . .

William Pickens, in the *Nation* of March 23, 1921, told of one additional note of consideration shown Lowry by his murderers: " . . . the Negro said never a word except when the mob brought his wife and little daughter to see him burning." Despite the fact that the plans for the execution had been widely published hours before the actual burning, not only was no attempt made to prevent the lynching, but Sheriff Dwight H. Blackwood of Mississippi County, in which Nodena is located, was quoted by the *Press* to the effect that "Nearly every man, woman and child in our county wanted the Negro lynched. When public sentiment is that way, there isn't much chance left for the officers. . . ."

Mississippi

"She was not sure, but thought he looked like the one who had attacked her," the Memphis *News-Scimitar* said of the attempted identification by a white girl in hospital when J. P. Ivy, a Negro, was shown to her in September 1925. That slender connexion was sufficient for a mob of Mississippians who, on Sunday, September 20, thus disported themselves. J. L. Roulhac, a reporter for the *News-Scimitar*, tells the story:

I watched a Negro burned at the stake at Rocky Ford, Miss., Sunday afternoon. I watched an angry mob chain him to an iron stake. I watched them pile wood around his helpless body. I watched them pour gasoline on this wood. And I watched three men set this wood on fire.

I stood in a crowd of 600 people as the flames gradually crept nearer and nearer to the helpless Negro. I watched the blaze climb higher and higher encircling him without mercy.

I heard his cry of agony as the flames reached him and set his clothing on fire.

"Oh, God; Oh, God!" he shouted. "I didn't do it! Have mercy!" The blaze leaped higher. The Negro struggled. He kicked the chain loose from his ankles but it held his waist and neck against the iron post that was becoming red with the intense heat.

"Have mercy, I didn't do it! I didn't do it!" he shouted again.

. . . Nowhere was there a sign of mercy among the members of the mob, nor did they seem to regret the horrible thing they had done. The Negro had supposedly sinned against their race, and he died a death of torture.

Soon he became quiet. There was no doubt that he was dead. The flames jumped and leaped above his head. An odour of burning flesh reached my nostrils. Through the leaping blaze I could see the Negro sagging and supported by the chains. . . . .

. . . The mob walked away. In the vanguard of the mob I noticed a woman. She seemed to be rather young, yet it is hard to tell about women of her type; strong and healthy, apparently a woman of the country. She walked with a firm, even stride. She was beautiful in a way. . . .

"I'm hungry," someone complained. "Let's get something to eat." . . .

In the same issue of the *News-Scimitar* was printed another story which reveals the truth of Walter Hines Page's warning of three decades before the burning:

"Gov. Whitfield won't have a lick of luck with any investigation of the burning of Jim Ivy." So declared William N. Bradshaw, of Union County, Mississippi, admittedly a member of the mob that for forty-eight hours sought the Negro accused of criminally assaulting a white girl near Rocky Ford, Miss., Friday morning in a statement to the *News-Scimitar* this morning. "And furthermore," he continued, "not an officer in Union County or any of the neighboring counties will point out any member of the crowd. Why, if he did, the best thing for him to do would be to jump into an airplane headed for Germany—quick. Sure the officers know who were there. Everybody down there knows everything else. We're all neighbors and neighbors' neighbors." . . .

Appropriately enough, Bradshaw's statement is captioned: "MOB MEMBER LAUGHS AT PROBE."

Had the Governor of Mississippi or any other officials wanted really to take action against the perpetrators of this horrible affair, they need not have depended upon the officers of whom Bradshaw spoke. The *News-Scimitar* published three "exclusive" photographs of the lynching, in which the faces of at least a hundred members of the mob are easily distinguishable. Yet the coroner's jury returned the expected verdict that Ivy had come to his death "at the hands of a mob, the members of which are unknown."

Georgia

"Southern chivalry" draws no line of sex. An unscrupulous farmer in south Georgia refused to pay a Negro hand wages due him. A few days later the farmer was shot and killed. Not finding the Negro suspected of the murder, mobs began to kill every Negro who could even remotely be connected with the victim and the alleged slayer. One of these was a man named Hayes Turner, whose offence was that he knew the alleged slayer, a not altogether remarkable circumstance, since both men worked for the dead farmer. To Turner's wife, within one month of accouchement, was brought the news of her husband's death. She cried out in her sorrow, pouring maledictions upon the heads of those who had thrust widowhood upon her so abruptly and cruelly.

Word of her threat to swear out warrants for the arrest of her husband's murderers came to them. "We'll teach the damn' nigger wench some sense," was their answer, as they began to seek her. Fearful, her friends secreted the sorrowing woman on an obscure farm, miles away. Sunday morning, with a hot May sun beating down, they found her. Securely they bound her ankles together and, by them, hanged her to a tree. Gasoline and motor oil were thrown upon her dangling clothes; a match wrapped her in sudden flames. Mocking, ribald laughter from her tormentors answered the helpless woman's screams of pain and terror. "Mister, you ought to've heard the nigger wench howl!" a member of the mob boasted to me a few days later as we stood at the place of Mary Turner's death.

The clothes burned from her crisply toasted body, in which, unfortunately, life still lingered, a man stepped towards the woman and, with his knife, ripped open the abdomen in a crude Cæsarean operation. Out tumbled the prematurely born child. Two feeble cries it gave—and received for answer the heel of a stalwart man, as life was ground out of the tiny form. Under the tree of death was scooped a shallow hole. The rope about Mary Turner's charred ankles was cut, and swiftly her body tumbled into its grave. Not without a sense of humour or of appropriateness was some member of the mob. An empty whisky-bottle, quart size, was given for headstone. Into its neck was stuck a half-smoked cigar—which had saved the delicate nostrils of one member of the mob from the stench of burning human flesh.

South Carolina

On a spring morning of 1925 a sheriff and three deputies set forth from Aiken, South Carolina, to arrest a Negro thirteen miles from town who was suspected of selling whisky. The four reached the house and found Sam Lowman away at the mill having corn ground into meal. Bertha Lowman, his twenty-seven-year-old daughter, and her mother, seeing the white men approach, started to enter the house. Coloured women in the South never feel at ease when white men prowl about their homes. The four white men, dressed in plain clothes and wearing no insignia of their official positions, ran to surround the house. The sheriff struck Bertha Lowman in the mouth with his fist. Her mother started to her daughter's rescue—and was shot through the heart by

one of the deputy sheriffs. A son and a nephew, plough-
ing in a field near by, heard the screams and shot, and
rushed to the rescue of the two women and several young
children who were within the house. In the firing which
followed, the sheriff was killed, and Bertha Lowman,
her brother, and her cousin were dangerously wounded.
According to their own testimony, the three deputies
swore that none of the Negroes was in a position to
shoot the sheriff—it seemed more than likely that he
met death from the gun of one of his own men.

The dead sheriff and his deputies were all members
of the Ku Klux Klan. Under its guidance the mob spirit
flamed high, and the trial of the three Negroes was far-
cical—the two boys were sentenced to death and Bertha
Lowman to life imprisonment. A Negro lawyer of Columbia, dismayed at the scant chance given the three for
life, successfully appealed their cases to the Supreme
Court of South Carolina. That tribunal promptly reversed the lower court, ordered a new trial, and re-
buked the trial judge, who, among other things, had
apologized for the lawyers assigned by the court to
defend the Negroes, explaining that they had been
obliged by the court to defend them, and not by their
own wishes.

A white lawyer of courage and decency from Spar-
tanburg aided the Negro lawyer from Columbia at the
new trial. So excellently was their case prepared and so
flimsy the evidence against the three defendants that

the judge was forced, fearing reversal, to grant a motion for a directed verdict of not guilty for one of the defendants. He was promptly re-arrested on a charge of minor importance and once again lodged in jail.

To the office of an Aiken attorney, recently elected to the state legislature, hurried a number of men. The result of that conference was seen when many men within the hour began hurrying towards Aiken, winter home of wealthy and socially prominent Northerners, from points even as far distant as Columbia, ninety miles away. About three o'clock in the morning a mob "overpowered" the jailer and the sheriff, who explained that he, wholly unaware of anything unusual in the air, had "just happened" to get up from a comfortable bed and walk to the jail. The three Negroes were taken to a tourist camp on the outskirts of Aiken, where some two thousand men and women were gathered. Sudden hope sprang into the breasts of the three victims as they were lined up, freed from their bonds, and told to run. Off they started—and a volley of bullets was pumped into their backs. The mob laughed loudly at the clever joke.

The two boys, one twenty-one and the other seventeen, fell dead. Bertha Lowman had many wounds, but none fatal. She squirmed in her pain over the cleared space of the tourist camp, upon which with faint brilliance the moon shone through the trees. The shifting target and the half-light cost the mob many bullets. "We had to

fire more than fifty shots at her before one of them
stopped her," was the story of one of the lynchers. A
spasmodic quiver—and the crowd, its work done, went
home to their beds.

". . . Death at the hands of parties unknown," said
the coroner's jury. Investigation by the National Association for the Advancement of Colored People disclosed that the charge against Sam Lowman of whisky-
selling was without foundation; that it had been made
in an effort to embarrass the owner of the land Lowman rented; that the sheriff and the jailer had not only
not resisted the mob, but had assisted in the lynching, as
had members of the South Carolina legislature, relatives
of the then Governor, lawyers, farmers, business men,
and politicians, and particularly members of the Ku
Klux Klan. To the Governor was furnished a full statement of the facts, with names and addresses of the
lynchers. The New York *World*, furnished also with
the information, sent one of its best reporters, Oliver
H. P. Garrett, to the scene and for thirty days featured
the story on its front page. Other newspapers, notably
several in South Carolina led by R. Charlton Wright of
the Columbia *Record*, waged an insistent campaign for
indictments and convictions. The incoming Governor,
John G. Richards, promised action. In January 1927
the grand jury refused, despite the evidence, to return
indictments. Governor Richards denounced the verdict

as "a travesty upon justice" and launched a vigorous campaign—against golf-playing on Sunday!

In September 1925 a mob of Georgians, not content with murdering sane Negroes, actually broke into the state insane asylum at Milledgeville and lynched a violently insane Negro who, in one of his periodic fits of dementia, had killed one of the nurses. Julian Harris, the most courageous editor of the South in attacking evil, said of the lynching of Dixon with characteristic directness in his Columbus, Georgia, *Enquirer-Sun:* "We first explain to the world that the Negro is a child, and then, when he commits a heinous crime, we lynch him as if he were a Harvard professor."

Expectant mothers, children, hopelessly insane, mental defectives, innocent or guilty—American mobs of recent years have drawn the line neither in the choice of their victims nor in the sadism of their deeds of death. One can easily comprehend the truth and depth of James Weldon Johnson's observation to the effect that "lynching in the United States has resolved itself into a problem of saving black America's body and white America's soul."

Yet, however, ghastly and depressing these pictures are, there were many signs that they are exactly what might eventually be expected. Towards the end of the

nineteenth century, when, almost imperceptibly, the
number of deaths with torture became increasingly frequent, there was little concern expressed at this sinister
change. Public indifference grew until such barbarities
were received with but momentary comment—barbarities which would have aroused far greater condemnation had they occurred, not in the United States, but in
Mexico, Soviet Russia, or China.

The roots of this sadism were long since planted in
American life. James Elbert Cutler in his *Lynch-Law*
cites only three burnings between 1830 and 1840. During the tense years between 1850 and 1860 there were
nine burnings, one of them of a woman accused of poi-
soning her master. The number gradually increased
after the Civil War, though the number recorded during
the Reconstruction Period was not high in proportion to
the number of victims. Cutler found burnings as follows
during the last two decades of the nineteenth century and
the first few years of the twentieth: 1884, Texas, one;
1891, Texas and Louisiana, one each; 1892, Arkansas,
one; 1893, Texas, one; 1894, Kentucky, one; 1895,
Texas, one; 1897, North Carolina, one; 1899, Georgia,
Mississippi, and Kentucky, one each; 1901, Kansas, one;
1902, Mississippi, three, and Arkansas, Texas, and
Colorado, one each; 1903, Illinois and Delaware, one
each; 1904, Georgia and Mississippi, two each.

One of the last-named cases reveals the increasing
sadism which began to manifest itself more frequently

about that time. The New York *Tribune* of February 8, 1904 tells of a double burning in Mississippi:

> Luther Holbert, a Doddsville Negro, and his wife were burned at the stake for the murder of James Eastland, a white planter, and John Carr, a Negro. The planter was killed in a quarrel. . . . Holbert and his wife left the plantation but were brought back and burned at the stake in the presence of a thousand people. Two innocent Negroes had been shot previous to this by a posse looking for Holbert . . . . There is nothing in the story to indicate that Holbert's wife had any part in the crime.

Benjamin Brawley, in *A Social History of the American Negro,* quotes the Vicksburg, Mississippi, *Evening Post*—which, obviously, can be relied upon not to add anything to the account of what actually happened—as to a new refinement introduced into the killing of Holbert and his wife—the use of corkscrews. This is the story:

> When the two Negroes were captured, they were tied to trees and while the funeral pyres were being prepared they were forced to suffer the most fiendish tortures. The blacks were forced to hold out their hands while one finger at a time was chopped off. The fingers were distributed as souvenirs. The ears of the murderers were cut off. Holbert was beaten severely, his skull was fractured, and one of his eyes, knocked out with a stick, hung by a shred from the socket. . . . The most excruciating form of punishment consisted in the use of a large corkscrew in the hands of some of the mob. This instrument was bored into the flesh of the man and woman, in the arms, legs and body, and then pulled out, the

spirals tearing out big pieces of raw, quivering flesh every
time it was withdrawn."

One may well imagine that death, even in the form of
burning at the stake, must have been welcomed gladly
by the man and woman as relief from such bestiality.
This is what Mississippians did, not only to Holbert,
who, at most, was guilty of killing his opponent in a
quarrel, but to Mrs. Holbert, who was innocent of any
connexion with the murder.

Georgia staged a double burning in the same year,
which aroused widespread discussion at the time. Paul
Reed and Will Cato, charged with the brutal murder
of a white family, had been duly tried, convicted, and
sentenced to death when the mob broke into the court
room, seized the prisoners, and burned them.

Here and there such episodes were repeated, mobs apparently vying with each other in devising more fiend-
ish methods of torture. By the end of the first decade
of the new century such orgies spread even as far north
as Pennsylvania. At Coatesville in that state in 1911
Zach Walker, a Negro, killed a constable in a fight in
which he also was severely wounded. Chained to a
bed in a hospital, Walker was taken out by a mob, bed
and all. Albert Jay Nock, in the *American Magazine*
for February 1913, told how the bedstead broke; how
Walker, wounded and helpless, chained to the lower
half of the hospital cot, was thrown on a pile of wood,

drenched with oil, and burned alive. "When Walker with superhuman strength," wrote Nock, "broke his bonds and tried to escape, they drove him back with pitchforks and fence rails and held him there until his body was burnt to ashes." And when a grand jury refused to indict the members of the mob, the lynchers were given an ovation.

During the same year a successful Negro farmer in Tennessee, who had by his prosperity aroused the jealousy and enmity of poor whites, was ambushed as he drove to town with his daughters to sell a load of cotton. The three were killed, the two girls by hanging and the father by shooting; the wagon was driven under the tree on which the girls' bodies hung, and fire was set to it, burning the bodies to a crisp.

Texas followed in 1912 with another burning. Dan Davis, a Negro charged with rape, was thus executed at Tyler. The St. Louis *Post-Dispatch* told how Davis calmly asked the mob: "I wish some of you gentlemen would be Christian enough to cut my throat." His request was in vain. Instead there was bitter disappointment, first because those entrusted with the task of starting the fire were deemed too slow, and second because not enough fuel had been provided. A few who dashed away to fetch more wood were rewarded with front-row positions.

Louisiana in December 1914 lynched three Negroes,

one of them, an aged Negro of excellent reputation, by slow burning. Even under extreme torture he refused to confess to the murder with which he was charged. Shortly afterwards the Houston, Texas, *Post* reported that all three victims had been found wholly innocent of the crime.

Fifteen thousand people including the Mayor, the Chief of Police, and many women and schoolchildren, witnessed the burning of a defective charged with the murder of the wife of his employer at Waco, Texas, in 1916. Tennessee furnished two particularly loathsome burnings in 1918—one at Memphis and the other at Estill Springs.

So the ghastly story runs. The number of lynchings was decreasing, but it may well be assumed that these terrible burnings, mutilations, and deeds too horrible for further detailing even in a study of lynching are doing more moral and psychological damage to their perpetrators than a greater number of victims executed by the more humane methods of hanging or shooting. When one notes the insidious growth of brutality which has made possible such abnormal, perverted crimes during the present century, one can see that the war cannot be blamed for the record of the past ten years, when, of 454 victims of Judge Lynch, sixty-six of them were killed with some form of torture. When, further, one connects with these the floggings, tarrings and featherings, mutilations, and other forms of mob violence other than lynchings which have plagued the South especially, and, to a lesser extent, other parts of the United States, within recent years in the wake of the Klan, one feels justifiable apprehension for the future.

I T IS exceedingly doubtful if lynching could possibly exist under any other religion than Christianity. Not only through tacit approval and acquiescence has the Christian Church indirectly given its approval to lynch-law and other forms of race prejudice, but the evangelical Christian denominations have done much towards creation of the particular fanaticism which finds an outlet in lynching. The responsibility of the Christian Church for mob-law against Negroes is not much less than its responsibility for slavery, for of all the great religions of mankind Christianity is the only one to draw the colour line and thus set up an elaborate array of invidious distinctions which assure the white Christian of his immense superiority. "Color was never a badge of slavery in the ancient or medieval world," says DuBois in *The Negro,* "nor has it been in the modern world outside of Christian states."

It was Christian nations in the eighteenth and nineteenth centuries that made African slaves supply the demand for cheap labour in Christian lands; it was Christian nations that despoiled Africa, and Christian Belgium that cut off hands and ears in the Congo; it

was Christian nations that sought as long as they possibly could, their own hands being stained, to avoid
recognizing the misdeeds of Leopold in the Congo and
to escape taking action to end his barbarities; and it is
Christian England and France and Italy that have their
iron heel upon Africa and India and China, and Christian America with hers upon the Caribbean nations
today. It is the Christian South, boasting of its imper-
viousness to the heretical doctrines of modernism, that
mutilates and burns Negroes, barbarities unmatched in
any other part of the world.

In permitting colour to be used as a cover and a justification of the emotions of cruelty which religious
fanaticism engenders, Christianity stands indicted
among the religions of the world. It is no accident that
in these states with the greatest number of lynchings
to their discredit, as is seen in the table on pages 248–
249, that the great majority of the church members are
Protestants and of the evangelical wing of Protestantism
as well.

For as long as religion has existed, which is almost
from the day when man first crawled upwards from
primeval slime and stood erect, religion has led not
only to acts of self-abnegation, nobility, and martyrdom, but has as well given birth to deeds of cruelty,
greed, and savagery almost beyond belief. The greatest solace man has known in times of sorrow or fear,
it has also, in the words of Lewis Browne in *This Be-*

lieving World, given birth to such pictures as this: "Men have slaughtered and ravished in Jerusalem because they had—religion. Men have gouged eyes and ripped bellies because they—believed! . . . Strange potency, this thing, we call religion. It has made men do barbarities beyond the reach of credence. For it men have done foulnesses below the foulness done even by beasts. . . ." And it is both axiomatic and understandable that whenever and wherever men have been devout to the point of fanaticism, their excesses, both of generosity and barbarism, have been in proportion to their devoutness.

That religion has inspired its adherents to deeds of frightful cruelty and of magnificent nobility is accepted. For reasons too numerous to be entered into here, colour and colour prejudice have profoundly influenced Christianity to a far greater extent than any of the other great religions. Skin colour in the United States has served as a focusing-point for much of the cruelty engendered by emotional religion in much the same fashion as in other countries Jews have been the target of pogroms. Foul pages in American history have been written by means of lynchings and burnings in those very states which most vociferously have adhered to evangelical Protestantism as represented by the Baptist and Methodist Churches.

How true this is can be seen by anyone who is even slightly familiar with the aftermaths of violently emotional revival services, when men and women are stirred to frenzy. It is a well-known fact that revivals and camp-meetings often produce an increase in hospital cases of mental disease. No person who is familiar with the Bible-beating, acrobatic, fanatical preachers of hell-fire in the South, and who has seen the orgies of emotion created by them, can doubt for a moment that danger-ous passions are released which contribute to emotional instability and play a part in lynching. Like periodic waves of insanity these evangelical disturbances have swept the South and the Middle West. Experts in men-tal diseases have long since established the danger of such revivals. However vigorously these preachers may exhort their hearers to abstract Christian principles and virtues, the human mind, its more violent emotions once loosed, does not always direct its actions into the paths urged. It is impossible to estimate the extent of the misdirection of such fanatical religious outbursts; but there can be no question that, however honest the preacher may be, the very violence of the emotions stirred up has contributed to release through lynching.

But, the objection may be raised, fanatics have stirred people before and Negroes were not chosen as victims. Why, therefore, should responsibility for lynching, however small, be laid at the doors of Methodists and Baptists and other emotional, hysterical, primitive re-ligions?

The answer lies in the prejudices, fears, and super-

stitions of the people whose emotions are released. In
Salem in 1692 religious fanaticism led to the choice of
"witches" as victims of persecution; in Seville eighty
years later the Holy Inquisition condemned a woman
to death by burning for practising the black arts; in
England sixty years earlier than the Seville episode
and in Germany twenty years afterwards there were
waves of religious persecution against so-called witches.

In the United States Protestantism has swung far
away from the teachings of tolerance and human broth-
erhood preached by Jesus and has become, in the
words of André Siegfried, "the religion of the Anglo-
Saxon or 'superior' race," in spite of "sincere protestations to the contrary." Such a course is seen to have been
practically inescapable when the history of the Church
during the two and a half centuries of slavery in
America is examined. Not only did the Church, by
adroit sophistry, dodge the issue of human bondage,
but theologians actually utilized the Bible and the teachings of Jesus Christ in defence of the system, and thus
committed the Church to a course and a point of view on
the question of race and colour which ever since have
afflicted it. Puritans in New England quieted their conscience over profits from the slave-trade by loudly proclaiming that their primary motive in bringing the African to the United States was to give him the blessings of
white civilization and Christianity. Hurd's *The Law of
Freedom and Bondage* tells of the general attitude in

squaring conscience with slavery: "Opposition to slavery was . . . largely stilled when it was stated that this was a method of converting the heathen to Christianity. The corollary was that when a slave was converted he became free. Up to 1660 it seemed accepted . . . that baptism into a Christian church would free a Negro slave. Masters, therefore, . . . were reluctant to have their slaves receive Christian instruction. . . . Virginia finally plucked up courage (in 1667) to attack the issue squarely and declared by law 'Baptism doth not alter the condition of the person as to his bondage or freedom, in order that diverse masters freed from this doubt may more carefully endeavor the propagation of Christianity.' "

The same state furnished a spokesman in the House of Representatives for a full theological defence of slavery, which is quoted by Charles and Mary Beard. The Virginia Congressman ended his lengthy plea in these words: "I believe that the institution of slavery is a noble one; that it is necessary for the good, the well-being of the Negro race. Looking into history, I go further and say, in the presence of this assembly and under all the imposing circumstances surrounding me that I believe it is God's institution. Yes, sir, if there is anything in the action of the great Author of us all; if there is anything in the conduct of His chosen people; if there is anything in the conduct of Christ Himself who came upon this earth and yielded His life as a sacri-

fice that all through His death might live; if there is
anything in the conduct of His apostles who inculcated
obedience on the part of slaves towards their masters
as a Christian duty, then we must believe that the institution is from God."

While such specimens of hypocrisy and sophistry
may cause a smile today, yet so far as the Negro problem is concerned, the Protestant Church in the lynching
states has changed fundamentally but little in the years
since such sentiments were voiced. The chief difference lies in the fact that so unblushing a defence of
slavery or of lynching would hardly be dared today.
But in so far as actions are concerned, the Church in
states like Mississippi has changed very little. If approval of lynch-law is not expressed as frequently or as
vehemently as it was twenty years ago, seldom is there
clerical condemnation of mob murder. Protestantism in
the lynching states has become the stronghold of bigotry, directing its onslaughts against Negroes, Catholics,
and Jews. It is no accident that William Joseph Sim-
mons, a Methodist lay preacher, should have been the
one to resurrect the infamous Ku Klux Klan. No especial shrewdness was needed by him and his fellow
workers to realize that Baptist and Methodist preachers
were the very best material for Klan organizers. William J. Robertson, himself a Southerner, in *The Changing South* declares that the post-World-War Klan "was
the direct result of the extra-Christian campaigning of

the so-called Christian brethren in the Methodist and
Baptist ranks." André Siegfried points out in his
America Comes of Age that the Klan drove in communities "run by a narrow-minded middle class and
inspired by a Protestant clergy. . . . The Baptist minister is usually in sympathy with the Klan and is often
appointed Kleagle or local publicity agent. When a
hooded band marches mysteriously out to offer a well-
filled purse to some worthy preacher, the choice . . .
falls . . . always on a Baptist or a Methodist."

The proclivity to join and spread the doctrine of the
Klan, "consecrated as Protestant to the teaching of the
Christian religion, and pledged as white men to the eter-
nal maintenance of white supremacy," was but a more
concrete evidence of white, Southern Protestantism
directed against the Negro; it was the organization
of anti-Negro sentiment which in the past had even at
times witnessed ministers of Jesus Christ leading lynching mobs.

Direct and extra-legal action against those who have
incurred the ill will of this ministry has long been the
rule in the South, whether it led to the tarring and
feathering of some man or woman who was suspected
of wrongdoing, the burning, as in Mississippi, of text-
books mentioning the theory of evolution, or finding expression in the rope or faggot. The people, held fast in
the grip of this ministry, have exemplified the soundness of the ancient Hebrew proverb; "As the people,

so the priests." Lacking the healthy sense of critical examination of religious beliefs, the South has largely been unable to smash or rationalize "the fervour, the intensity, the passion back of the assertion that the South holds aloft the torch of Anglo-Saxon ideals, racial integrity, and religious purity." Unrestrained, unintelligent emotions have given rise to varied forms of intolerance which have retarded the South's mental development. Self-imposed standards of ritual scrupulousness and conformity to ancient precepts; opposition to attendance of Southern students at Northern universities for fear that their faith might be undermined there; the tendency of more intelligent and independent-minded men to enter other professions than the ministry add to the seriousness of a situation in the South which is acute enough in an age of scepticism in all parts of the country.

Against such a background the efforts of a few courageous ministers towards a more humane, intelligent attitude towards the Negro stand out as miracles. The vast majority indirectly and directly have fed the passions of the lynching mob and helped pile up the shameful number of mob murders. Lynchings seldom occur where there is enlightenment. The holding fast to outworn and faulty ideas, the retention of ignorance with all its vicious by-products, provide the fertile soil from which springs the rule of the mob, whether it be one to burn a Negro or flog a white woman or to wage a cam-

paign for compulsory reading of the Bible or to enact
an anti-evolution law. Intolerance can grow only in the
soil of ignorance; from its branches grow all manner of
obstacles to human progress.

Against this depressing picture of an ignorant, prejudiced, intolerant ministry waging relentless warfare
upon the colleges and universities, stirring up racial and
religious antagonisms to the point of frenzy, dominating
state legislatures and newspaper columns, what is there
of hope? The answer to this question is not reassuring
either to the South or to the Negro. Yet there are a few
signs of light, faint it is true, but still worthy of hope.

First there is the exceedingly revolutionary change
for the South of a spirit of honest scholarship, of in-
quiring scepticism, which is being seen in some of the
Southern universities and which is challenging the absolute dominance that the Church has so long held over
these institutions. The University of North Carolina is
by far the most outstanding of these; Vanderbilt University, Tulane, and the University of Georgia are following in somewhat modified fashion.

Second there is the beneficial effect of the farce enacted at Dayton in 1925 during the Scopes trial. Critics
of the course pursued by the defence attorneys, including
even so astute an observer as Professor Siegfried,
have questioned the wisdom of riddling the late
William Jennings Bryan by means of ridicule. These
critics have said that the puncturing of the smug com-

placency of Bryan and the exposure of the imbecility of some of his beliefs deified Bryan in the eyes of those who believed with him. That may be true, but it also is probably true that these would never have changed their minds had Bryan not been exposed. The net effect of the whole trial has been to make the more backward states of the South exceedingly sensitive to ridicule, so that a number of Southern legislatures which were on the point of passing anti-evolution measures have by one means or another evaded doing so. More important, a keen interest has been created, not only in evolution, but as well in other subjects heretofore forbidden. There is to be seen here and there in the South evidences of the birth of a tendency to scrap many of the old ideas and to form new ones in line with the development of modern science and enlightenment. This includes even the hitherto dogmatic beliefs and assertions concerning race. Here and there the light begins to break through.

The growing industrialism of the South, though bringing its own problems, is tending to wean away adherents from the Church and widen the horizon of those who come into contact with the newer order. It is no wonder that the embattled fundamentalists are fighting so lustily—even the most stupid of them cannot fail to realize that their reign ends when intelligence gains a foothold.

There are some signs of hope in changes that are taking place in the theological seminaries of the South.

A prominent Southerner who, perhaps more than any other man, has had the opportunity of seeing what is going on among the various denominations writes: "There has been an increase in the attendance of theological seminaries in the South since the War and my observation is that the men are of somewhat better calibre than those who were in the seminaries before the War. It may have always been, it has certainly been true within the last twenty years, that the men of the most initiative who enter these seminaries rarely ever remain long in the pastorate. . . . It is encouraging, however, to remember that up to ten years ago white theological seminaries never gave any consideration whatever to the racial situation in the South. It was never mentioned when I was in school and I waited until I was out of the University to discover that the race question was one of the severe tests of our so-called 'ethical ideas.' That is not true today. Most of the seminaries are giving some serious attention to the question and many of them are giving it very thorough attention. On the whole, the young men who are coming out of the theological seminaries are of the liberal type. . . . The younger ministers . . . are very superior to the older ones.

"Whenever I speak to the Methodists or Baptists I almost always preface my remarks with some sort of careful statement regarding 'social equality.' If I do not—it matters not what I say about Negroes or lynch-

ing, 'social equality' is about the first thing they think
of and it makes them go into a sort of insane rage. The
Methodists now are worse than the Baptists. This is not
true of the Episcopal or Presbyterian Church. . . .

"The most hopeful element in the church situation
is the fact that women are coming into a larger and
more effective place in the life of the church. Women,
having recently come through their struggle for representation and self-expression, are very sensitive to any
situation that denies this to others—hence, in the
churches of the South, the group most sensitive to the
race situation is the women. . . ."

Even the most honest Southerner, familiar with the
appalling ignorance of the great majority of ministers
in the South, both urban and rural, may feel that these
steps are on a scale with the proverbial attempt to bail
the Atlantic Ocean with a tea-spoon. Contrasted with
the great ignorance of the past and the absence of efforts towards more enlightened attitudes on race and
other controversial subjects, however, these efforts give
evidence of a new tendency which is hopeful. At present
the incubus of a narrow, prejudiced ministry, relieved
only by a few men of higher calibre, presents the South
with one of its most serious problems. Hope of a more
enlightened type of religious leader, who will lead the
South from the paths of mobbism and resistance to enlightenment and to decency, does not rest in the present
generation of ministers. As death and age thin their

ranks and the effect of the efforts now beginning towards greater liberalism becomes evident, then and
only then will Protestantism in the South turn from its
advocacy of mob-law, its crippling of universities, its
opposition to knowledge, and its handicapping of Southern mentality.

CHAPTER FOUR

SEX AND LYNCHING

WITH the most intransigent Negrophobe it is possible to conduct a conversation on certain phases of the race question and do so with a measured calmness of manner. But when one approaches, however delicately or remotely, the question of sex or "social equality," reason and judicial calm promptly take flight. Berserk rage usually seizes one's conversational *vis-à-vis*. One can count with mathematical certainty upon the appearance of the fiercely challenging: "How should *you* like to have your daughter marry a nigger?" as the answer to any attempt at sane discussion of this phase of the race question. It is of no avail to point out that there is but a tenuous connexion between sex relations or intermarriages on the one hand and ordinary justice and decency on the other. Sex with all its connotations so muddies the waters of reason that it is impossible to bring the conversation back to its more unimpassioned state.

Of all the emotional determinants of lynching none is more potent in blocking approach to a solution than sex, and of all the factors, emotional or otherwise, none is less openly and honestly discussed. Even the most

fair-minded Southerner keeps away from the topic, fearing the tempest which follows its introduction as a topic
of discussion. As a result, this element in the race problem and specifically in lynching is distorted by the conspiracy of semi-silence into an importance infinitely
greater than the actual facts concerning it would justify.
From the time of its introduction as a defence of lynching, which, as we shall see, was simultaneous with the
elevation of cotton through inventions to one of the
premier crops of the world, sex and alleged sex crimes
have served as the great bulwark of the lyncher.

Some years ago in a novel I ventured to put into the
mouth of one of my characters, a Southern white lawyer, what seemed to me a simple and truthful statement to the effect that not in all the lynchings where
rape or attempted rape was alleged had such a crime
actually occurred. Down upon me tumbled an amazing volume of abuse from small-town newspapers of
the South. One of them, a Georgia daily, indignantly
asserted that the South is the most law-abiding section
of the United States, and, a few paragraphs later, invited me to visit Georgia and see what "Southern gentlemen do to those who slander the fair name of Southern womanhood."

This Southern excitability over so universal a fact as
sex has many causes. It is impossible to trace them all
to their source. But a few of them can be separated
from the fabric of many patterns and weavings which

is the race problem. Perhaps statement of these may serve to bring some light where there has been little but heat.

There are at least a half-dozen reasons why sex harasses the South, and especially the rural South and the anti-Negro South. The first is one that is common to most regions which are predominantly rural—the dullness of life and the lack of such diversions as theatres, moving-pictures, parties, concerts, shop-windows, and the like, which in the city leave less time for concupiscent desires and thoughts. The South has suffered more than other section because of the fact noted in the preceding chapter—the preponderance of Methodists and Baptists to whom such diversions as card-playing, dancing, and theatre attendance are forbidden. In many parts of the South this circumstance has elevated attendance at church, sex escapades, and lynching into the principal escapes from the grim and sordid reality of work.

A second reason for over-emphasis on sex in the lynching states is that the creation of the bogy of sex crimes as a defence of lynching has made the South the terrified victim of the fears of its own conjuring. Despite the evidence of the figures showing that only a small percentage of lynched Negroes were even accused of rape, the vast majority of whites in the states where lynchings are most frequently staged really believe that most mob murders are the results of sex crimes. Having

created the Frankenstein monster (and it is no less terrifying because it is largely illusory), the lyncher lives
in constant fear of his own creation and, at the same
time, has by means of his creation caused more crimes
against the women of his race than there would have
been in a more sane and normal environment.

The vast amount of advertising which lynchings have
given to allegations of sex crimes has induced subnor-
mal Negroes to attempt crimes of rape, the power of
suggestion being as potent as it is. Such an aftermath to
lynchings has been noted in certain instances—the idea
of successfully consumating sex crimes having been im-
planted by the news of a lynching. The mentally deficient individual who would thus be impregnated with
the thought of being able to escape punishment would
obviously not be deterred by fear of a horrible death
in expiation of his crime. Thus it is not at all improbable
that lynching has added to sex crimes or attempts at
such crimes. There is some foundation for such a surmise when one considers how infrequently Negroes are
charged with such crimes in the states where lynchings
have been very infrequent.

Third in the list of causes of sex-obsession in the
South is the Southern white woman's proneness to hysteria where Negroes are concerned; and this is an
aspect of the question of lynching which needs investigation by a competent psychologist. It is appropriate
here only to report observations and conclusions based

upon a fairly extensive experience with the statistics
and literature of lynching. My own experience in in-
vestigating forty-one lynchings and the study of several
thousand others reveals that in the great majority of
cases where rape or attempted rape was alleged, the
women can be divided into four classes: young girls
ranging from the ages of twelve or thirteen to nineteen
or twenty years of age, passing through the difficult
period of adolescence; second (and this includes a considerable percentage of the alleged victims of attacks),
women who range in age from the middle forties upwards; third, women who have been married for many
years and usually to rather unattractive husbands;
fourth, spinsters.

Fourth among the reasons is the intense religiosity of
the lynching states and the primitiveness of their religion. Psychologists have long since established the intimate relation between the emotions of sex and of
religion, and that the more primitive the religion, the
greater is the part played by sex. Critics of the American scene from Frances Trollope to H. L. Mencken have
observed in the frenzy of Methodist revivals what comes
dangerously close to being a species of sex indulgence.
Certainly one can find in many parts of the South numerous counterparts, male and female, white and Negro,
of the woman William James describes in his *Varieties
of Religious Experience* who could induce a state of

rapture by dwelling upon the thought that "she could always cuddle up to God."

It is also a familiar phenomenon that the sex instinct figures in religious ecstasy in somewhat the same proportions that illiteracy and ignorance afflict the religious-minded. Given an elaborate system of taboos that label as "sinful" even relatively innocent diversions, which would absorb at least a part of the time otherwise given to erotic thoughts and desires, subjected to the explosive experiences attendant upon religious experiences, deprived by ignorance, geographical isolation, and poverty from books and other intellectual releases, and victims of a bogy of the Negro as a *bête noire*—all these handicaps reveal vividly the state of mind which turns devout Christians into lynchers, especially when sex enters the equation.

Maynard Shipley, in his *The War on Modern Science,* quotes the observations of a Southern observer on the connexion between illiteracy among native-born whites and the preponderance of Baptists in the total church population of certain Southern states. "The U. S. Census report for 1920 shows that the percentage of illiteracy is highest in those states where Baptists are more numerous. Among the native-born whites alone the percentage of illiteracy runs as follows; Alabama, 6.3; Georgia, 5.4; Kentucky, 7; Louisiana, 11.4; Mississippi, 3.6; North Carolina, 6.8; South Carolina, 6.5;

Tennessee, 7.3; Texas, 3; Virginia, 5.9; West Virginia, 4.6." Cochran compares these figures with those of such states as Connecticut, New York, the Dakotas, and others in the North and West where there are fewer communicants of the evangelical churches and where also the illiteracy rate of native-born whites is one-half of one per cent. He paints a depressing picture of the relations between the poverty of ministers and their congregations, the ignorance of the clergy, the extent of Fundamentalism and opposition to scientific advancement among them, which seem amply to justify the pessimistic declaration of J. R. King of South Carolina that the common people of his state are "fast losing their thinking faculty for lack of use. Generations of religion have produced a generation of religious fanatics. . . . Unless there is help from the outside, the South is headed for a darker period than the Dark Ages."

When the student of human behaviour views the Southern scene and especially the rural sections of the South and sees the extent of religious bigotry of which the Ku Klux Klan, the Bible Crusaders, and the Supreme Kingdom are the organized forms; when he sees such catch-phrases as "Back to the Rock of Ages and forget the ages of Rocks" raised to the dignity of a supreme rallying-cry of fanaticism; when he watches the resolute efforts of the embattled Fundamentalists "who are making dogma into a statute and are driving out all who preach and teach the modern view of the Bible and religion" and thereby make even more primitive the religion of the South; when he sees all these and other forms of religious intolerance gripping the lynching states, then he can understand one of the most potent reasons for the enormous emphasis on sex in these states. Even a superficial knowledge of the history of early and primitive religions will cause him to understand the insane fury of the residents of rural Mississippi and Georgia and Texas and the extent of their sadism when real or alleged sex crimes are perpetrated.

Dr. A. A. Brill, the distinguished psychiatrist, even more definitely links propensity to mob violence to abnormal sex instincts. "The torture which is an accompaniment of modern lynching," he declares, "shows that it is an act of perversion only found in those suffering from extreme forms of sexual perversion. Of course, not all lynchings are conducted in this fashion, but it is not uncommon to read accounts telling that the victim was tortured with hot irons, that his eyes were burned out, and that other monstrous cruelties were inflicted upon him. Such bestiality can be recognized only as a form of perversion. Lynching is a distinct menace to the community. It allows primitive brutality to assert itself and thus destroys the strongest fabric of civilization. Anyone taking part in or witnessing a lynching cannot remain a civilized person." (Quoted from *Tenth Annual Report* of the N. A. A. C. P.)

A fifth reason for preoccupation with sex in the lynching states is the traditional attitude towards coloured women and the price now being paid for that attitude. For two and a half centuries of slavery slave women had no control over or defence of their bodies. As chattels, their bodies were their own only in so far as their owners were men of moral integrity. In codes and practices these owners ranged from those who permitted neither themselves, their overseers, nor male members of their families to tamper with the persons of their female slaves, down to owners who deliberately used slave women as breeders of half-white slaves—combining, as it were, pleasure with business. Midway between these poles of conduct were those who permitted and even urged their sons to take Negro mistresses and thus protect the chastity of white women, a somewhat analogous practice to that of ancient Rome when Solon caused female slaves "to be brought to the city and exposed to save other women from assaults on their virtue."

Whatever may be the current interpretation of virtue, it is axiomatic that an individual or society cannot maintain for any great length of time dual standards of personal conduct which are diametrically opposed to each other. The man who attempts to maintain a fixed respect towards one group of women and indulges meanwhile in all manner of immoralities with another group may seek ever so hard to maintain such a balanced dual standard. Inevitably and imperceptibly he finds it impossible, to the detriment of his respect for the first group. And that is precisely what has happened to the South, the white South, both male and female. For more than two hundred years this moral deterioration has affected the Southern states, and from that decay arises the most terrifying of all the aspects of the race problem to the white man.

As far back as 1691 the number of children born of slave fathers and white women had increased so alarmingly that Virginia, which seems to have been usually the state to legislate against what appeared to be evils arising from slavery, sought to end this intermixture by means of a law which prohibited *marriage* between a white man or woman with "a Negro, mulatto, or Indian man or woman, bond or free," on pain of banishment; and which prohibited *sexual relations* between a *white woman* and a *Negro* or *mulatto*. The care exercised not to interfere with sexual relations between *white men* and *Negro or mulatto women* will be noted. Any white woman who bore a Negro's child was liable to be fined or, in default of payment of that fine, to be sold into service for five years; the child was "bound in servitude to the Church wardens until thirty years of age."

Maryland even earlier (in 1663), faced with the same problem, passed a law declaring that any freeborn (i. e., white) woman marrying a Negro slave should serve the slave's owner as long as her husband

lived; children born of the union should also be slaves,
the property of the owner of the father of those children. The effect of this law was dismaying to its fram-
ers. Slave-owners, with eyes solely upon profits, utilized
the measure to secure slaves free of all cost and urged
their Negro male slaves to marry white women—thus
securing the wives as slaves and the children they bore
to their husbands free of all cost.

Even a later law, passed in 1715, making any free
Negro and white woman who married each other servants for seven years and their children servants until
thirty-one years of age did not put a stop to this type
of marriage. North and South—wherever there was
slavery—the loose conduct of white men towards coloured women was finding its counterpart in relations
between white women and coloured men. Neither legislation nor public condemnation seemed appreciably to
check intermixture of this sort. As the Northern states
for economic reasons abandoned slavery, the practice
and the problem seemed to dwindle in extent, but upon
the states of the South, which, also for economic reasons clung to and extended slavery, there was placed a
social heritage—and a fear—which have not yet been
shaken off.

That the white women involved in this intermixture
were not always of the humbler sort is revealed in an
interesting decision of the South Carolina Supreme
Court rendered in 1831 (*The State* v. *Thos. D. Davis*

and *The State* v. *William Hanna; 2 Bailey*, 558). These cases are to this day the leading ones in South Carolina on the question involved and have been subsequently cited and followed in such cases as *Blake* v. *Tisdale* (14 *Rich Equity*, 100); *State* v. *Cantey* (2 *Hill*, 615); *Johnson* v. *Boon* (1 *Speers*, 270); *Waite* v. *Tax Col. of Kenshaw District* (3 *Rich.*, 140); and *Davenport* v. *Caldwell* (10 *S. C.*, 335). The issue involved in the two cases first cited was the credibility as a witness of a mulatto and the Supreme Court decision defined a mulatto, quadroon, person of colour, and a person with so little Negro blood as to be deemed in law a white person. In the course of its opinion the South Carolina Supreme Court made two interesting statements bearing upon the nature of intermixture in that state, which read: "In each case the jury found the mother to be a white woman and she was accordingly admitted to be sworn as a witness. . . . It is certainly true, as laid down by the presiding judge, that 'every admixture of African blood with the European, or white, is not to be referred to the degraded class.' "

In some states the idea of a child of a white woman being a slave was so repugnant that laws were passed defining such a child born of a Negro father as "Free Issue" and decreeing that such offspring should be free. In brief, the type of Southern white who was not above taking a Negro mistress was saddling upon himself and others a fear which to this day is the most serious men-

ace to peace and amicable settlement of the race problems. Tannenbaum in *Darker Phases of the South* says
of this class: "You cannot indulge in certain relations
toward colored women and expect to escape free from
influence in your attitude toward white women. The
idealization of the white women in the South is thus
partly the unconscious self-protection on the part of
the white men from their own bad habits, notions, beliefs, attitudes, and practices. This helps to give the
facts of sex in the South their peculiar quality of sensitiveness. It is not insinuated that all white men in the
South are habituated to practices suggested here, but
there are enough of these men to give the atmosphere
its requisite tensity."

This defensive mechanism of which Tannenbaum
speaks finds expression as well in the derogatory attitude towards coloured women of which a classic example was a Southern office-holder who declared that
there was no such thing as a virtuous coloured girl of
more than fourteen years of age; and who at the time
possessed a considerable family by a Negro mistress as
well as one by his white wife. In truth, there would be
considerable amusement in the attitude thus expressed
if it were not so tragic—a member of a supposedly
"superior" race explaining and excusing his own moral
derelictions by emphasizing the "immorality" of the
women of the "inferior" race.

This type of Southerner is largely responsible for the

sixth and by far most vexing cause of sensitiveness on
the subject of sex in the lynching states. There is probably no single statement more frequently or more vehemently made in the South than that there is an ineradi-
cable repulsion between the races which will keep the
two races eternally separated. Even if there were not
the evidence of possession of white blood by so large a
percentage of Negroes, the very violence of this assertion and the frequency with which it is repeated would
cause an unbiased observer to wonder why the statement is worthy of being made at all if those who make
it believe it. Professor André Siegfried, of the Paris
École des Sciences Politiques, in *America Comes of
Age* gives the reason for the vehemence of the assertions. He says that "although the whites declare that the
Negro is physically repulsive to them, you know that
it simply is not true."

Though Professor Siegfried refers particularly to
lack of physical repulsion of white men towards coloured women, much more disturbing is the suspicion
that the absence of repulsion applies to both sexes of
both races. There is no doubt that most of the intermixture has come from relations between white men
and coloured women. But the suspicion that it is not
confined to that class motivates to a large extent the
sadistic features of many lynchings and burnings. It
has caused the enactment in twenty-nine states of anti-
intermarriage laws—legislation which would be most

unnecessary if the boasted repulsion were really true. It has led—human curiosity overriding as it does laws, conventions, customs, and edicts of all sorts—to experimentation, most of which might not have been thought of had there not been the challenge of a barrier. It has caused the surreptitious spreading of stories of Negro superiority in sex relations and it did not matter whether or not that rumoured superiority existed in fact or fancy—the very violence of opposition by the mobbist seemed to lend credence to the truth of the assertion. Once again the lyncher brought into being a condition diametrically opposite to that which he sought to attain.

Though this terrifying thought is kept as a sort of racial secret, there are those who occasionally commit the indiscretion of saying what they think. There is, for example, the Rev. C. A. Owens, an eminent white Baptist minister of North Carolina, who, according to the Winston-Salem, North Carolina, *Journal*, preached a sermon in that city in 1925 in which he gave his reasons for believing in and supporting the Ku Klux Klan. The *Journal* quoted Mr. Owens in part as follows: "With the present movement northward of Negroes and in the absence of a race prejudice that has protected the Southerners, there is the greatest possible danger of the mingling of the races, so that in the future it may come to pass that you will send your daughter to the North for culture and she will come back with a little Negro."

Seldom if ever has there been a greater "slur upon

the fair name of Southern womanhood" than this intimation by the Reverend Mr. Owens that only Southern race prejudice is keeping white women from sex
affairs with Negroes. Perhaps it is fortunate for Mr.
Owens that he is neither a Northerner nor a Negro—he
most certainly would have been threatened with violence
if not with lynching for such a statement had he not
been a Southerner and a Klansman.

And then there is John Powell of Richmond, Virginia. A pianist and composer whose chief claim to fame
rests in his adaptation and rendition of Negro music,
his *Rhapsodie nègre* being one of his best-known works,
Powell became alarmed if not terrified when he discovered that the comforting idea of an absolutely pure
white race with unmixed Nordic blood coursing through
its veins was largely a myth, especially in Powell's own
Virginia. He joined with others of similar fears, and,
largely as a result of their efforts, there was introduced
into the Virginia legislature in 1925 an amendment to a
so-called "racial purity" law enacted the previous year.
This amendment shifted the burden of proof that white
Virginians were all-white from the individual to the
State, added to the penalties Virginia legislatures had
been enacting for two hundred and thirty-five years
against illicit intercourse between the two races, for-
bade whites and Negroes even to sit together in places
of public assembly (with characteristic impudence this
was aimed at Hampton Institute, for the education of

Negro and Indian youth, which receives but an infinitesimal fraction of its support from white Virginians), and called on Congress to deport Negroes to Liberia.

With the exception of the blow at Hampton Institute none of these provisions was especially new. The section which revealed the perturbation in the minds of the sponsors was that which required all citizens of Virginia to register with a State Bureau of Vital Statistics all of the racial strains, however remote, which had entered into their families. To arouse public support of the measure Powell and his confreres, with commendable energy if not discretion, unearthed an immense amount of evidence of intermarriage and miscegenation in Virginia, some of it affecting some of the most respected families of the state.

One of Virginia's most conservative daily newspapers —the Richmond *Times-Dispatch*—served Powell's purpose by printing and editorially endorsing twelve articles written by Powell on his discoveries. In its issue of February 16, 1926 the *Times-Dispatch* said of the articles: "They are authentic, and the instances to be cited are based on accurate knowledge following personal investigation or on official records in the office of Dr. Plecker, the State Registrar of Vital Statistics."

With such assurances from a conservative Southern newspaper, backed as it is by official records of the state, it may be assumed that the facts are beyond all question correct. There can be no suspicion that some

meddling outsider is responsible. In truth, the same
paper published on March 2, 1926 a letter from a correspondent regarding Powell's revelations in which the
statement is made that" . . . where formerly mulattoes
were born almost entirely of Negro women, there are
now as many or more born of white women."

Here are a few of the cases which Powell and the
Virginia Bureau of Vital Statistics revealed:

In Henrico County a young white woman, enceinte,
was taken by her cousin to a nursing-home for the de-
livery of her child. The man told the matron that he
loved his cousin despite her condition and wanted to
marry her. When born, the child was obviously a Negro.
Grilled for some time, the mother finally broke down
and made a written confession, which Powell quotes
in part. Let Powell tell the story. "She stated that the
father of her child was a middle-aged Negro. . . .
'God put love into our hearts,' she writes, and describes
how both of them fought against the voice of God. She
concluded, 'His face may be yellow, but his heart is
the heart of a pure white gentleman.' The matron de-
plores the increasing frequency of such cases."

Powell, who throughout his articles combines the role
of preacher with his other occupations of social re-
former and musician, moralizes: "Every detail of this
story is replete with nauseous horror. Nothing could
be more indicative of the decadence of racial pride
and the insecurity of the color line." One may be quite

certain that none of Powell's horror is caused by the circumstance that the state of Virginia, in having made marriage between the two who loved each other a crime, forced the birth of a bastard.

Powell's next shocker comes from the proud city of Richmond. "A young girl of excellent family and high social position met a young man who came to Richmond from one of the counties of the state. She was attracted by his unrestrained gaiety and high spirits and amiability. . . . They became engaged. Before the engagement had been made public, friends of the girl's family heard rumors that the young man was Negroid, told her tactfully what they had heard, and urged her to make thorough investigation before proceeding with the marriage. She rejected their advice and the wedding was celebrated. . . . Shortly afterward, the rumor was fully confirmed, but the marriage relation was not disturbed."

Powell adds: "This case, with another, almost identical, occurring in another wealthy and prominent family in Richmond, shows that wealth and social position are not proof against the danger. . . . Similar material is on record at the Vital Statistics Bureau from Richmond and from seven of the eight counties of the district."

From Dinwiddie County Powell reports this case: "A wealthy farmer, who, although a self-made man, is married to a woman of refinement and culture, lost his

mother a few years ago. The neighbors came to the funeral. There appeared also Negroes, claiming to be
his brothers and sisters. They were apparently accepted
as such. After the ceremony, the neighbors demanded
an explanation. The reply was, 'Wall, I'm a white man.
My mother and my father were both white, and I'm
their legitimate offspring. These Negroes are illegitimate children born to my mother after my father's
death.' " Powell, still the exhorter, adds: "It is impossible to conceive anything more appalling than this
case, or more indicative of the precarious condition of
the color line." Or, we might add, of the precarious
condition of a sense of appropriateness or good taste.
Perhaps the novelists who have pictured Virginians as
the epitome of good breeding and courtesy did not
know all Virginians.

Historic Westmoreland County, birthplace of George
Washington, supplies the industrious Powell with his
next case. "A white woman," he reports, "mother of two
children left her husband for a Negro man. After two
years, she returned to her family, bringing with her a
mulatto child to which she had given birth. Her husband received her and the mulatto child, and re-
established her as the head of the household. Other
children were born to her, some white and some colored, her husband apparently making no protest. . . .
The enormitous [sic] consequences of racial integrity
of this case are inconceivable, and no attempt will be

made to suggest them. . . . These cases may be taken as typical of conditions which, though limited as to numbers, are general enough to geographical distribution throughout the district."

On February 23, 1926 Powell revealed by means of the *Times-Dispatch* a number of cases from the Fifth Congressional District of Virginia which included eight counties, and Charlotte, birthplace of Patrick Henry and John Randolph. Among them is a case which reveals the extremes to which fanaticism will go. A child was born to a white couple, but "after a few days presented the typical appearance of a Negro. The parents were devastated by grief and humiliation, as both had, until now, believed themselves and each other to be white. Nevertheless, they kept their heads and instituted a searching genealogical investigation, which established the fact that through the mother the child was *one two-hundred-and-fifty-sixths Negro*." (Italics ours.)

Powell reports also a conversation regarding one of the counties in the same congressional district. "A member of the House of Delegates and a State Senator were recently discussing the situation in this county. 'I estimate that at least one-third of the white population of X County are more or less Negroid.' The Senator replied; 'You put it too low. I should say at least one-half.' "

From Loudon County, Eighth Congressional District, Powell reports the birth of a supposedly legitimate child to a white couple. "Previous to the birth of the child, the mother had been staying in Washington and had been intimate with a Negro. The child was born after her return to her husband. It is a typical mulatto." A similar case from Louisa County is reported in the same article.

These are but a few of Powell's authenticated cases from Virginia alone. In the twelfth and last article, captioned: "Summary and Conclusion," Powell concludes his revelations with these soothing and consoling words to his white fellow-Virginians: "The color-line in America has been more permanent than in any other instance in history." Perhaps he is right.

Powell, described by a newspaper correspondent as "the dark-skinned agitator for a 101 per cent, lily-white," saw his pet measure quietly done to death in the Virginia State Senate. The lower house had passed the bill, but wiser heads in the Senate discovered that if the measure became a law, a considerable number of eminent Virginians, living and dead, would be classed as Negroes. The state of Georgia has recently passed a somewhat similar bill. Perhaps the example of Virginia caused the legislature of that state to enact such a law, but to neglect to provide funds for its enforcement.

One is able to understand, thanks to Powell and racial purity advocates of his type, why fear plays so prominent a part in the pother over sex in the lynching states. If such conditions can be true in a state like Virginia, with its heritage of achievement and culture, what, one wonders, can be the situation in the states of the far South? In one of them there was an attempt some years ago to pass a law defining as a Negro any person with even an infinitesimal fraction of Negro blood. A member of the legislature who later became nationally known for his tirades against the Negro, by means of which he was time and again elected to high office, defeated the measure when he declared that its passage "would bathe the state in blood."

All of these reasons for the dominance of sex as a factor in lynching, with all their other complications, centre in one objective—the economic ascendancy over Negro labour. William Pickens, the brilliant Negro scholar, rightly terms it "simply the shrewdest battle cry of the forces seeking the economic domination of the Negro. . . . The average man, even the most brainless, may be moved by it," and thus sex is used as "a red herring . . . whenever one discusses the economic, political or civic advancement of the Negro." In an address before the Sunrise Club of New York in 1926 Mr. Pickens laid down four propositions in the relation of "the sex-bogey to the real interests of society." They are (1) that the sex cry is always associated with economic greed and is loudest wherever the oppression and robbery are the worst; (2) that race or colour antagonism is not "instinctive," as is evidenced by little children and by unspoiled races, and as is often amusingly shown by the relationships of the dominant race to its servants from among the dominated race; (3) that there are no biological barriers between any two of the so-called human "races" and that pseudo-scientific demonstrations of the subject could be used in one direction as well as in another, and could be made to prove anything; and (4) that while sex, or "racial integrity" is very convenient publicity material for the leaders of American lynchings, sex-attachment is in fact one of the smallest causes, among even the alleged causes of this most barbarous form of repression. In these four concise statements is included as complete a statement as is possible within such limits of the relationship between sex and lynching.

If those who commit and defend lynchings on the score of its necessity as protection of womanhood were sincere and intelligent, there are certain immediate steps possible for them which would do more towards ending racial intermixture than ten thousand burnings.

The first of these would be the repeal of the laws forbidding intermarriage which today are on the statute books of twenty-nine states.[1] To dispose of the disadvan-

---

[1] These states, according to the 1927 *World Almanac* are: Alabama, Arkansas, Arizona, California, Colorado, Delaware, Florida, Georgia, Idaho, Indiana, Kentucky, Louisiana, Maryland, Mississippi, Missouri, Montana, Nebraska, Nevada, North Carolina, North Dakota, Oklahoma, Oregon, South Carolina, South Dakota, Tennessee, Texas, Utah, Virginia, and West Virginia.

tages of such laws to Negroes they deprive coloured women of legal protection of their persons or redress should a white man seduce one of them; they place upon coloured people the implication of inferiority which self-respecting Negroes resent; they give legal sanction to belief by a certain type of white man that despoilment of a coloured girl is not so reprehensible as a similar offence against a white girl. Such laws severely handicap the struggle which Negroes are making—it is they more than anything else that is checking intermixture. In many smaller towns of the South protection of women of their race from the unwelcome advances of white men can and sometimes does mean lynching for the protectors. Governor Hugh M. Dorsey of Georgia in 1921 gave an example of such conditions which is not unusual. He had called together a group of prominent citizens of that state to place before them a hundred and thirty-five cases of mistreatment of Negroes within the state which had come to him unsolicited during the preceding two years. Case No. 1 reads:

"July, 1919, two white men, drunk, went to the Negro section of a town in this county at night. An elderly Negro got his gun and went into the streets, it is claimed, to protect the women of his race. In the shooting, which followed, one of the white men was killed.

"The Negro was placed in the jail. The sheriff left him there, *with no guard*, to go to another place to get a prisoner. A county commissioner hearing that a mob was coming went to the jail to remove the prisoner, but could find no key to unlock the door. *The mob had the key.* They lynched the Negro." (Italics ours.)

So much for the disadvantages to Negroes of anti-intermarriage laws. For whites there are many harmful aspects. It obviously is not best for the moral stamina of any race to grant legal immunity to its men when they commit sex crimes against the members of another group. It is especially bad to grant such immunity to the men of a section that has had so bad a moral career as has the South. It is true beyond all doubt that there are many men and women in the South who not only are bitterly opposed to the victimization of coloured women, but are themselves morally clean. It is likewise true that their number is infinitely small when compared with white Southerners who, while innocent of such offences, do not feel that there is as great turpitude attached to seduction or rape of a coloured girl as of a white girl. Double standards of this sort have a most vicious effect upon morals, and anti-intermarriage laws perpetuate and protect such double standards.

There is no scientifically exact method of determining precisely the effect of anti-intermarriage laws upon the number of mixed bloods born in states where there are such laws and in states where there are not. The figures of the United States Census Bureau are not taken seriously by careful students because the term "mulatto" as used by that bureau is not a biological classification, but only a convenience for the use of the enumerators. There is also the factor of interstate migration, which plays a considerable part in nullifying the value of the census figures.

For lack, however, of more accurate figures, the decennial reports of the Census Bureau offer interesting data on the effect of laws prohibiting intermarriage between whites and Negroes. Even after most liberal allowances are made for the interpretations given by the individual enumerators to the departmental definition of mulattos, whites, and pure-blooded Negroes; even after making further allowance for interstate migration; even with due allowance for the reluctance of some Negroes to admit the possession of white blood, a significant circumstance emerges from these reports. The increase of mixed bloods in relation to the total of unmixed Negroes is considerably higher in those states which forbid intermarriage by law between whites and Negroes than in the other states, where no such prohibition exists. "Shot-gun weddings" or seduction and bastardy prosecutions have an extraordinarily salutary and moral effect upon certain types of men. On the score of efficiency anti-intermarriage laws have been a failure.

Such laws also actually compel and increase bastards. Powell, in his story of the girl and man into whose hearts "God put love," is not the only one who knows of such cases. These states, by banning marriage in such instances, force sordid, clandestine affairs and the bearing of illegitimate children with all the disadvantages which such offspring suffer in modern society. The only humane, sensible, and decent thing to do is to remove the barriers to marriage, and thus insure proper care of the children born of such unions.

Over and above all these immediate results is the psychology which such laws induce. There will never be any lasting solution of the race problem so long as laws and custom permit and sanction notions of superiority and inferiority which exist only in the imaginations of the self-elected "superior" group. To these states one feels inclined to give unsolicited advice— that instead of fuming and fretting over sex they should cast aside petty fears, realize that neither laws nor customs are of much avail where two individuals are drawn to each other, and that their frantic efforts to prevent intermixture are doing more than any other thing to cause intermixture, usually upon the lowest plane.

CHAPTER FIVE

THE ECONOMIC FOUNDATIONS
OF LYNCH-LAW

ISCUSSION of lynching began and continued with,
and is today made up almost wholly of arguments
that the practice is necessary to save white women from
rape. A mere casual examination of the circumstances
which attended the birth of lynch-law and of those which
have run concurrently with its career will demonstrate
beyond all doubt that the charge of sex crimes is a red
herring for the obfuscation of those who would ordi-
narily think clearly upon and be opposed to such barbarism.

*Lynching has always been the means for protection,
not of white women, but of profits.* That this is true can
be seen by scrutiny of the facts from the time lynching
began to become an integral part of our national folkways to the present day. For the sake of clarity the history of lynch-law can roughly be divided into four
periods. The first of these begins about 1830 and ends
with the outbreak of the Civil War; the second begins
with Appomattox and covers the period of Reconstruction; the third starts about 1890, when imperialism centring in Africa became a fixed policy of white European

nations and the United States, and ends with the outbreak of the World War; and the fourth covers the years from the beginning of hostilities in Europe to the present time.

To understand the economic roots of lynching it is necessary that the difference be made clear between lynching prior to 1830 (and in certain parts of the far West after that date) and lynching as it is today. This difference is most clearly seen in the circumstances under which the practice, as far as we know, began. The generally accepted and most credible version of the inception of lynch-law attributes the doubtful honour to Charles Lynch, a Quaker, born in 1736 in what is now Lynchburg, Virginia. Lynch was a man of considerable importance in his community and a member of the Virginia House of Burgesses. In the years immediately preceding the Revolutionary War the activities of the American patriots in their struggle for freedom from England were greatly hampered by the Tories. This was especially true of that section of Virginia where Lynch lived; and he and his fellow patriots were further harassed by notorious characters who utilized the unsettled state of affairs to indulge in proclivities for horse-stealing and other crimes. The nearest trial court was two hundred miles away and reached only by means of frequently impassable and dangerous roads. Conferences between Lynch and men of his class resulted in the formation of an extra-legal court of which Lynch was chief magistrate. Two of his neighbours sat with him. The accused was faced with his accusers, permitted to give testimony on his behalf, and allowed to summon witnesses, and in every possible way his rights were safeguarded. If acquitted, he was allowed to go free, with apologies and often with reparation. If found guilty, he was given "thirty-nine lashes on the bare back, and if he did not then shout 'Liberty Forever!' " hung up by the thumbs until he did so. Only rarely was an accused person sentenced to death.

So also was ready justice dispensed by the Vigilantes and other similar extra-legal bodies in the period when Western states were first being settled. Here, too, courts of law and the machinery for the apprehension and punishment of criminals were either few or non-existent.

Out of this form of extra-legal punishment of criminals has grown the practice of modern mobs of seizing, condemning without even a semblance of a trial, and executing persons accused of crimes in communities where the excuse cannot be offered that there are no courts of law. As has been pointed out, this type of lynching began simultaneously with the industrial revolution. How and why this should have been so can be seen by viewing the effect of that revolution on the institution of Negro slavery.

For more than two centuries the success of slavery had been dependent almost wholly upon the extent of the supply of free, fertile, and level land. The planting aristocracy had rapidly exhausted the soil, not bothering to replace through fertilizers and intelligent tillage its pristine fertility. Instead the slave power had spread its territory by moving on to new land. Such a short-sighted and rapacious policy had led inevitably to an increasingly insistent demand for new land, and Texas and the Floridas were acquired by the United States in highly questionable fashion as a result of the demands of the slave states. Meanwhile the less fertile land of the Northern states had caused the early abandonment of slavery for the more profitable pursuits of trade and manufacturing.

But despite the acquisition of new land slavery was beginning to prove a highly unprofitable business, and in many parts of the South slave-owners were freeing their slaves, not because the system was morally wrong, but simply because it no longer paid. Then—Eli Whitney invented the cottin-gin and, in the words of Charles and Mary Beard, "smashed an old economy created in the childhood of the race—challenging the spinners at their wheels in New England and the cotton planters with their armies of slaves far away under the burning sun of Mississippi and Louisiana." Arkwright's spinning-frame, Watt's condensing steam-engine, the fly shuttle, the carding-machine, the power-loom, came into being, and, by means of them all, cotton became

overnight, as it were, one of the premier crops of the
world as the demand for it leaped ever higher and
higher.

As cotton mounted in value, belief in the justice and
necessity of Negro slavery revived in the cotton-growing
states. The inventions of Whitney and the others took
the cotton from the moment it was picked and swiftly
turned it into marketable and valuable material; no
invention appeared to eliminate physical labour in the
actual raising of the crop, nor has much yet been done
in that direction. Cotton was then, and is today, a crop
which to a large extent can only be raised by hand, and
a bountiful supply of cheap labour was necessary if the
demands for cotton were to be met.

All notions of abolition of slavery were quickly abandoned and every possible effort was exerted to end the
spreading of abolitionist sentiment and especially of
slave revolts. It was at this point that the lyncher entered
upon the scene as a stalwart defender of the slave-
owners' profits. The *Liberator* of October 1, 1831, for
example, tells of a man named Robinson who was
lashed on the bare back at Petersburg, Virginia, for
saying that "black men have, in the abstract, a right
to their freedom," and who was ordered to quit the
town and never return lest he be treated "worser." Winfield Collins, a passionate defender of slavery and
lynching, says in *The Truth About Lynching* of the period beginning in 1830 that "the excited state of the

public mind in some instances may have suspected plots of insurrection when none existed. However that may be, wherever and whenever such a plot was discovered, investigation nearly always pointed to the abolitionists as instigators. Indeed, even when Negroes were insubordinate and refractory on a plantation, it was often found that they had been tampered with by abolitionists. Occasionally, when such things were proved against an abolitionist beyond the possibility of a doubt, he would be immediately hanged to the limb of some convenient tree. Several were so dealt with in connection with the insurrection in Texas. As a rule, however, when the proof was not so conclusive, a severe whipping, or a coat of tar and feathers, would be given him, and then he would be forcefully admonished to leave the South." Collins naïvely adds: "One cannot but reach the conclusion that the anti-slavery agitation was detrimental to the happiness and welfare of the slaves, and to the free Negroes as well."

Each year that passed saw the practice of lynching (the term now tending more and more to mean the death of the victim) spreading to all parts of the slave states. The number of victims increased in direct proportion to the growth of the demand for cotton and to the growing sentiment in other parts of the country that slavery was not only morally wrong, but economically unsound. The false bloom of health that inventions had given the system—causing the annual cotton crop to mount from a mere two million pounds when Washington was president to more than two billion pounds in 1860, an increase which brought the cotton-raising states during the latter year alone some two hundred million dollars—blinded those who had given no attention to anti-slavery enthusiasts when slavery had not paid. It was this very circumstance which led to every available means of repression of those who sought to end slavery and which accounts for the rising tide of mob murders during the three decades which began in 1830 and ended with the outbreak of the War of the Rebellion.

So, too, did it lead to the introduction of calumny against a race in the efforts to justify the wanton mob-murders which were being committed. It is worthy of careful reflection that the Negro's alleged propensity for sex crimes was unheard of in the United States prior to 1830, although the first Negroes were brought to America in 1619. In 1710 there were 50,000 Negroes in the country; 220,000 in 1750; 740,000 at the time of the Revolutionary War, of which 700,000 were scattered on isolated plantations in the South; and 1,500,-000 in 1820. During all of these two centuries charges of rape against Negroes were unknown, although there was ample opportunity for commission of such crimes. Such accusations were made only *after* a defective economic system had been upturned and made enormously profitable through inventions and in doing so had caused slave-labour to become enormously more valuable. Charges of rape were made with increasing frequency as a greater number of lynchings and more brutal methods of execution of the victims brought vehement condemnation of lynching from other parts of the country.

Collins thus explodes in a burst of lyric frenzy in defending lynch-law: "The Negro, son of a wild and tropical race, content for thousands of years to roam the jungles of Africa, supplied by a bountiful nature with all his heart's desires, failing thus to develop any controlling trait of character, or mental stamina, and although civilizations rose and fell beside him, it meant nothing to him . . . and even now in the midst of American civilization he is moved to action, mainly, by gusts of primitive emotion and passion."

Passing over the "gusts of primitive emotion and passion" which find expression in the Ku Klux Klan and mobs that mutilate and burn human beings alive, one notes that Collins is speaking of the Negro of today, three hundred years removed from "the jungles of Africa." One wonders why champions of lynching never attempt to account for the fact that for two hundred years, nearer by a century to Africa than now, Negroes neither showed nor were accused of showing a propensity for sex crimes to any greater extent than any other of the races in the population of the United States. Cutler in his notable *Lynch-Law* seems not to have noticed the emergence of charges of rape at this time. Though

a meticulous student, he merely remarks that after
1830 lynching became more frequent in the South "for
the purpose of putting down abolitionism." He thus no
more than skims the surface of the underlying changes
in the economic order which made the doctrine of abolitionism so dangerous to those who practised lynching.

One need only glance at the figures to see how determined was the effort to prevent at all costs any freeing of the slaves. Morally indefensible and economically
unsound, the system of slavery forced its champions
to resort to brute force—always the last refuge of those
who can defend their positions in no other fashion. Cutler tells of three cases between 1830 and 1840 of burnings. Two of the victims were burned at Mobile,
Alabama, after a court had sentenced them to death for
the murder of two children. Collins puts it: 'The gentlemen of Mobile . . . seized the Negroes . . . and
burned them." A third victim during this decade was a
free Negro at St. Louis who, in helping another Negro
to escape being carried back into slavery, shot and
killed one officer and wounded another. When the matter came before the grand jury of St. Louis County,
Judge Lawless—by name and by interpretation of law,
fittingly named—instructed the jury to return indictments if the burned Negro was killed by "the few . . .
and, compared to the population of St. Louis, a *small*
number of individuals"; but to take no action if the
victim was found to have met his death at the hands of

many. "If," this amazing charge ended, "the victim
came to his end at the hands of the multitude, in the
ordinary sense of those words—not the act of numer-
able and ascertainable malefactors, but of congregated
thousands, seized upon and impelled by that mysterious, metaphysical, and almost electric phrenzy, which,
in all nations and ages had hurried on the infuriated
multitude to deeds of death and destruction—then, I
say, act not at all in the matter—the case then tran-
scends your jurisdiction—it is beyond the reach of
law." For denouncing this infamous plea for non-action
against the lynchers the printing-press of the famous
abolitionist, the Rev. E. P. Lovejoy, was destroyed by
the mob and he himself later killed at Alton, Illinois.

William Lloyd Garrison's *Liberator* and *Niles' Register* were the only journals of the period that attempted
to keep even fairly accurate and complete records of
the deaths at the hands of mobs during this period. The
former in its issue of December 19, 1856 recorded the
lynching during the preceding twenty years of "over
three hundred white persons." Cutler is of the opinion
that during the period "there were no doubt many cases
of the administration of summary justice in the remote
districts during the thirties and early forties which
never came to the notice of either *The Liberator* or
Niles' Register. . . . There is, however, abundant evidence to make the conclusion a safe one that lynch-law
was more and more resorted to during this period."

The reason for the rise of mobbism is obvious—the·
tide rose in an exactly parallel curve to the wave of
economic forces against slavery and of Northern sentiment which was at work to put an end to slavery. As
the slave-holders saw the fight going against them, despite their desperate struggle to check these forces,
they more and more resorted to the rope and the faggot. During the decade beginning in 1850 the obviously incomplete records cite the lynching of twenty-
six Negroes for killing their masters. Nine of the
twenty-six, one of the nine a woman, were burned at
the stake. During the same period twelve Negroes were
lynched for rape, four of them being burned alive.
There were other Negro victims charged with lesser
crimes, but the total of all Negroes lynched seems by
all records to be well below that of white victims.

Here, too, economic forces were at work, this time
to the advantage of the Negro. As a slave the Negro's
body had a definite, ascertainable cash value, precisely
as had an acre of land, a bale of cotton, or a horse.
Being merchantable, Negroes when accused or suspected
of crime were given the benefit of careful scrutiny of
the evidence of their guilt before execution by a court
or by a lynching mob. There are on record numerous
instances where the owners of lynched slaves sued for
and received damages for the loss of their property.
White bodies, on the contrary, had no market value,
and thus it was natural that prior to the Civil War

more white victims than Negroes came to their death at the hands of lynchers.

Economic interest not only acted as a deterrent in saving Negroes from lynch-law during pre-Civil-War days; it likewise saved Negroes from doing the more dangerous tasks. In Southern seaport towns and along the Mississippi white men were often used to load and unload ships. Barrels and other heavy objects sometimes came hurtling down, crushing the hapless who chanced to be in their path. Black men were too valuable to be risked in such fashion.

Frederick Law Olmstead in his *A Journey in the Seaboard Slave States in the Years 1853–1854* tells of an interesting case of this nature. A Virginia planter had an Irish gang draining swamp lands for him, though he was certain that Negroes would have done twice as much work. "He was sure they [the Irishmen] must have 'trifled' a great deal," Olmstead writes, "or they would have accomplished more than they had. He complained much, also, of their sprees and quarrels. I asked why he should employ Irishmen, in preference to doing the work with his own hands. 'It's dangerous work (unhealthy?) and a negro's life is too valuable to be risked at it. If a negro dies, it's a considerable loss, you know.' "

We now come to the second phase of lynching—the years of the so-called Reconstruction Period. The lynching industry was revolutionized by the Emancipation Proclamation, which wiped out the cash value of a Negro. The balance swung so sharply that it was not long after Lee had surrendered at Appomattox before Negroes formed the great majority of the lynched. So wanton and widespread were the murders, particularly after the Ku Klux Klan was organized, that the misconception arose that lynching did not begin until after the Civil War. Surprisingly enough, even such a student as T. J. Woofter, Jr., makes such an assertion in his *The Basis of Racial Adjustment.*

However, in a hasty glance at the panorama of lynch-law, the fury of mobbism during the Reconstruction era almost justifies this belief. Numerous factors contributed to this gory epoch. There was, of course, the psychological effect always created by wars. The loosing of murderous passions always ends in the glorification of the most proficient killer. There was, too, the fact that the South, though beaten, was far from convinced of the unrighteousness of her cause. There soon sprang up a host of legends of a largely fictitious ante-bellum South composed of courtly, goateed, mint-julep-imbibing gentlemen, of ravishingly beautiful and virginal women, of stately, porticoed mansions, and faithful, contented, singing "darkies," unspoiled by wicked abolitionist notions of any special merits of freedom over slavery. Such apparently harmless myths soon created a sense of inordinate suffering and a natural bitterness towards those who had ended so idyllic an existence, however non-existent in reality that life had been. Instead of listening to the sound advice of such men as General Robert E. Lee to accept the verdict of Appomattox and set about rebuilding the South in accordance with the demands of a changed and changing world, the opiate of dreams of "the lost cause" and the direct action of the Ku Klux Klan were adopted. Though there was much talk of restoring white supremacy and protecting womanhood, here, too, the motive back of the terrible reign of lynch-law was economic. For the vast majority of the whites of the late Confederacy—even of those who had owned no slaves—were united in a single cause—to re-enslave the Negro as far as was humanly possible.

The Report of the Congressional Commission of 1872 appointed to investigate the activities of the Ku Klux Klan gives a ghastly picture of the extremes to which resort was had to gain this end. The results of the inquiry fill thirteen volumes, each containing about six hundred pages. It would be difficult in all history to parallel the bloody record thus set forth. In Alabama alone there were 107 lynchings in less than two years. Within a few weeks in 1868 more than two thousand persons were murdered, assassinated, or "handled" by mobs in Louisiana, the bodies of 120 Negroes being found in Bossier Parish of that state following a "nigger hunt." The then Governor of Mississippi was cited as authority for the statement that in his state within two years beginning in April 1869 there were 124 lynchings. For an eighteen-month period beginning in January 1866 there were in North and South Carolina 197 lynchings. In nine counties of South Carolina within six months the Klan lynched thirty-five persons besides whipping, mutilating, or otherwise outraging men and women, white and black, who had incurred the Klan's ill will. "Partial returns" from Texas for a period from the end of the war to 1868 disclosed 1035 lynchings. Tennessee mobs staged 168 lynchings in the year ending July 1, 1868. Many of these lynchings were conducted with a bestiality unfit for publication.

I make no effort to minimize the difficulties which the white South and the black South faced after the Civil War. Yet it is only within very recent years that fair-minded historians, many of them Southerners, such as John Wade of Georgia (as in his life of Longstreet), are determining even approximately the truth of the Reconstruction era. The idea is slowly being abandoned that the post-Civil-War Negro governments, with all their mistakes and crimes, were so bad as such virulent Negro-haters as Thomas Dixon and his type have declared through printed and spoken word and the cinema. And it will probably be many more years before the South will cease deluding itself and face the fundamen-

tal economic motive of the reign of lynchings and mob-
bings and the efforts to justify such murders through
stories of Negro crimes and incompetency. For, as Du-
Bois states, "the white South feared more than Negro
dishonesty, ignorance and incompetency, Negro hon-
esty, knowledge, and efficiency."

In its efforts to re-enslave the Negro and make him
economically impotent the South of the Klan destroyed
one of its greatest assets and for economic reasons
whipped up violent passions which have not yet died
down. This asset was the healthy, life-giving antagonism
between the so-called poor white and the master class.
Prior to the Civil War the poor whites had suffered
from slavery but little less than the slaves. They had
been forced to till mountainous or otherwise unfertile
soil, all the level, well-watered, and fertile land being
taken by the slave-owners. These, in turn, feared the
poor white and were as apprehensive of the rise of a
white peasantry as "a peril to property, liberty, and
the Constitution" as they were of slave revolts. The
poor whites were denied the ballot, were denied education for their children, and in many places were not
allowed to enter churches for worship until the slave-
owners and their families had taken their seats. It was
no accident that one of the strongest blasts against slavery should have been written by Hinton Rowan Helper,
himself a poor white. For Helper along with many,

many others in the same condition saw that as long as there was Negro slavery, so long could whites too poor to own slaves be shunted off into poverty, ignorance, disease, and death.

The Emancipation Proclamation changed all this and placed master and poor white upon the same economic level. From that state came unification of a far more vicious sort—union in a common hatred and fear of the Negro. Belying their boasted racial superiority, both classes, panic-stricken, rushed into movements like the Klan, the White Camelias, and others organized for the same purpose—to "put the Negro in his place." Gone was the old dissent. Douglas Freeman, editor of the Richmond *News-Leader*, speaking of the present South, says: "Forced to think alike politically, many ceased to think at all." His statement might apply as well to every other phase of post-Civil-War life in the South, for there was a common complex against the Negro which coloured all thought and gave birth to bitter passions that fed the flame of mobbism and led to victims by the hundreds of rope and faggot.

The allegations for which Negroes were lynched rapidly widened in scope. Not only were they murdered by mobs on charges of murder and rape, but for miscegenation, "incendiary language," jilting a girl, unpopularity, refusing to turn State's evidence, being too prosperous for a Negro, "introducing smallpox," to prevent evidence, for testifying against a white man, talking back to a white man, and for every sort of petty offence.

The overthrow of the Negro governments and the removal of federal troops in no wise changed this order of things, but instead intensified the bitterness. Practically every Southern state passed labour and vagrancy laws; "the former masters, working through state legislatures, restored a kind of servitude by means of apprentice, vagrancy, and poor laws." Other discriminatory laws aimed at the Negro and his suppression appeared as the years passed—disfranchisement laws, "Jim Crow" car laws, statutes to prohibit common assemblage in school and even in church. As the forerunner of such efforts to humiliate, oppress, and re-enslave the freedmen, the lyncher's rope and torch appeared.

Other economic forces at work outside of the South contributed to the success of these efforts. There had been far from a united North against slavery and for the war between North and South, as the draft riots in New York showed. The war over, the North was well content to leave the Negro to his fate at the hands of his former masters and the poor whites. The notorious failure of the Freedman's Savings Bank, through which Negroes were robbed of some three million dollars, is an excellent example of indifference in the North to the Negro's future.

This indifference was only in part due to hostility to

the Negro. Congress had passed in 1862 the Homestead Act, which opened vast areas of fertile land in the West; it also had given land, subsidies, and other aid towards the construction of the Union Pacific Railroad, which linked the Atlantic and the Pacific. This action of Congress, together with discovery of silver, copper, lead, and coal in the West, had turned the attention of the North away from the South, and worked more largely towards relegation of the South to the national background than had the defeat of Southern arms. New inventions in the fields of electricity, aeronautics, railroad construction and operation, telephonic and telegraphic communication, farm machinery, and the automobile had contributed to a dynamically changeful and profitable era—an era of corporations rather than the old individual efforts, and the building of the huge Vanderbilt, Astor, Carnegie, Morgan, Rockefeller, Gould, and Frick fortunes, which would have astounded and dismayed Thomas Jefferson, less than a century before. All this contributed to a preoccupation in the North which shunted the Negro and the South into the limbo of unpleasant and forgotten things, and there were few who knew or cared what the lyncher's rope and torch betokened or masked.

The Age of Imperialism

If lynch-law fixed its roots in American soil in the thirties, forties, and fifties, and plunged those roots to the very lowest layer of the national and especially the Southern soil during Reconstruction, its full flower was destined to be seen as the nineteenth century entered its last decade. Not only was economic exploitation based upon colour of skin to be seen in the United States, but its spread was rapid throughout the world.

As though it had not already enough burdens to contribute to its ignorance and moral decay, there entered into the life of the South demagogues such as Cole Blease of South Carolina, Hoke Smith of Georgia, Vardaman of Mississippi, and "Pitchfork" Ben Tillman, who made as their sole platform hatred and vilification of the Negro. Lynching spread as far north as Omaha; in the South it sank to levels of barbarity unequalled since the days of the Klan. In 1892 there were 235 lynchings, of which 156 of the victims were Negroes; the following year there were an even two hundred; in the decade between 1890 and 1900 there were 1780 *known* lynchings.

No excess seemed too terrible for the mob. In Louisiana a fifteen-year-old girl was hanged after horrible deeds upon her; in Arkansas a Negro charged with rape was burned, the victim of his alleged attack being forced against her will to light the funeral pyre; Tennessee, Texas, Georgia, Mississippi, and other states of the South witnessed bestialities that shocked the entire country and the world. The Populist Party had just waged a shortlived but prosperous campaign in the

South, which threw terror into the Democratic Party. The lyncher and the legislator, the latter through disfranchisement laws, joined hands to eliminate the Negro from politics and thus prevent the possibility of the Negro's holding the balance of power. This was the death-blow to the hope of salutary political life in the South.

Coupled with fear of the Negro politically was fear of the Negro's economic progress. Three decades after Appomattox a new generation of Negroes was beginning to make itself heard. The ex-slave, whom the South professed to love so tenderly, was passing. Uncle Tom's sons and daughters were attaining manhood in more than the sense of years lived. Education and economic progress were bringing a new racial attitude into the Southern situation which was most distasteful to those who had owned slaves or who believed in the highly idealized fiction of a mythical pre-Civil-War South. Poor whites, fed by years of oily flattery after the Civil War had emancipated them and given them power and the vote, liked the emerging Negro no better than did the former slave-owners. As the machine age tended towards greater and greater standardization of houses, clothes, motor cars, editorials, and thought, the Southern white in his attitude on the race problem easily took the lead in becoming an automaton. Gerald W. Johnson, the brilliant Southern writer, summed up in a phrase the Southern political attitude that permeated all Southern thought. In the *Virginia Quarterly Review*

of July 1925, he wrote of the slavish, unthinking allegiance of Southern whites to the Democratic Party and
summed up the situation thus: "Had Beelzebub been
the Democratic nominee, the clergy would have been
deprived automatically of the privilege of the franchise,
and no doubt many of the laity also would have laid
down the ballot unused; but I have a strong belief that
the stalwarts would have rallied by tens of thousands
and gallantly gone to hell."

Perhaps the net effect of such sectional narrowness
upon the whites, and one of the causes of increased
bitterness against Negroes which found expression in
the mob, can best be seen in the matter of farm ownership. Poverty, the ravages of the boll-weevil, disastrous
rainy seasons, unintelligent farming resulting in ex-
haustion of the soil, combined with the great demand
for cotton, led to the stultifying one-crop system and
to the wasteful and often viciously abused sharecropping and tenant-farming systems out of which
peonage developed. Negroes were lynched, or intimidated and cowed when not killed, for daring to question
this exploitation or seeking to elude the clutches of
rapacious landlords, merchants, and bankers. A notable
instance of this was the famous race riot of 1919 in
Phillips County, Arkansas, in which upwards of two
hundred Negroes were slain by mobs, and a number of
the survivors were saved from legal lynching only
through a five-year legal struggle waged by the National

Association for the Advancement of Colored People.

In his *Darker Phases of the South,* Frank Tannenbaum told of the effect upon whites and Negroes of this economic system and revealed one of the reasons for the increase of bitterness between poor-white and black peasants. Quoting from bulletins of the Universities of North and South Carolina, Tannenbaum showed that whites were retrograding into the class of tenants far more rapidly than Negroes, among whom, despite migration, farm ownership was rapidly increasing. Two-thirds of the tenants are whites who have become "propertyless, homeless migrants"; in the cotton and tobacco area one-half of all the farms are occupied by white tenants. In the thirteen cotton-producing states, the University of South Carolina points out, "61.5 per cent. of all tenants are white, and only 38.5 per cent. are colored." In brief, despite the prosperity and bustling activity of the cities such as Birmingham and Atlanta, the majority of Southern whites in the rural South were and are sinking into an economic morass which makes them the prey of Klan organizers, anti-evolution mountebanks, mob hysteria, and every manner of charlatanry. Negroes, on the contrary, despite all the handicaps of ignorance, poverty, and oppression, have steadily added to their wealth and education and have become in many respects superior to the whites. At the close of the Civil War, Negroes operated twenty thousand farms; by 1922 the number had grown to upwards of one million, of which slightly more than half were owned or were being bought by those who operated them. This progress of a supposedly inferior race was one of the most fruitful sources of mob violence as acquisitions in this and other fields became noticeable towards the close of the nineteenth century. The total of 1780 lynchings during the last decade of the century was, in large measure, the mob's effort to check this rising tide of economic independence.

The already complicated Southern and national situation with regard to the race problem was further influenced, directly and indirectly, by a new world-attitude towards coloured peoples and especially towards Negroes. World imperialism centring in Africa led to a persistent, organized campaign of disparagement of those with dark skins, which rapidly changed the old attitude of indifference. A propaganda as subtle as it was vicious was utilized among white nations to prove the superiority of all things white and thus to justify a rapacious exploitation of non-whites. Only the cynical-minded noted that the souls worth saving and the minds capable of absorbing "white" civilization were those races which possessed lands or other things of great value. At the close of the Franco-Prussian War, only one-tenth of Africa was under nominal European control; at the turn of the century only Liberia and Abyssinia, comprising approximately 390,000 square miles, were free, while Great Britain, France, Germany, Spain,

Italy, Portgual, and Belgium between them controlled a total of 11,106,011 square miles. Coloured races in other parts of the world also felt the iron hand, not always velvet-gloved, of imperialism—dark peoples in India and China and the Caribbean Sea. This exploitation, in the words of DuBois, "transferred the reign of commercial privilege and extraordinary profit from the exploitation of the European working class to the exploitation of backward races under the political dominance of Europe. For the purpose of carrying out this idea the European and American working class was practically invited to share in this new exploitation, and particularly were flattered by popular appeals to their inherent superiority to 'Dagoes,' 'Chinks,' 'Japs,' and 'Niggers.' "

This was done through a number of methods—through the appeals of missionary societies for funds to bring Jesus to the poor, benighted heathen; through newspaper editorials and magazine articles and books. Of them all none was so potent or so successful as the sudden popularity of the theories of a mythical being called an Aryan, which Comte Arthur de Gobineau had given the world some years before the age of exploitation gave point to his theories. From Aryanism and its offspring—Anglo-Saxonism, Teutonism, Celticism, Nordicism—nations and white races found comfort and warrant for their imperialistic designs. Frank H. Hankins in his *The Racial Basis of Civilization* tells in these words how it was done: "In recent times doctrines of racial superiority have played an almost unsurpassed rôle in the larger politics of states. They have justified cruelty and inhumanity; they have constituted a basic assumption in the expansion of Europe and the growth of modern imperialism; they have stirred race hatred, aroused the sentiment of patriotism and fanned the flames of war. The astounding megalomania of the Germans of recent tragic memory has found its counterpart in certain elements of the national egotism of all other world powers."

Sir Phillip Gibbs's summary of the Versailles Conference gives another aspect of the fruit of this dangerous race hatred: "The old politicians who had played the game of politics before the war, gambling with the lives of men for territories, privileged markets, oil fields, native races, coaling stations, and imperial prestige, grabbed the pool which the German gamblers had lost when their last bluff was called and quarrelled over its distribution."

Thus the two went hand in hand—exaltation of all things white and the shameless robbery of those who were not white—and the end is not yet in sight, despite the terrible war that but lately ended. For the megalomania that finds expression in national and racial egotism was nowhere more evident than in the United States, where the Ku Klux Klan, the Nordics, and the lynchers are but the more obvious examples of that egotism. The lyncher during this epoch learned, with gratitude, that his efforts to exploit and oppress the Negro not only were not wrong but were, instead, a part of the task assigned to him by reason of his whiteness of skin. More, he found that criticism of his acts was dying down—for certainly those whose hands were not spotless could hardly afford to be too critical of others. The terrific impact of this whole propaganda against coloured races has penetrated far deeper than is visible on the surface. Not even a great world war, growing out of the prejudice and greed which this propaganda was so largely instrumental in creating could arouse the world to the gravity of continuing such a course.

Too busy developing its own vast resources, the United States did not join in the scramble for land in Africa. But the new century had not long been ushered in before American imperialism practised on coloured races began—through loans by the house of Morgan and other New York banking houses to Great Britain at the time of the Boer War, which helped extend British supremacy in Africa, and to the Japanese for furthering their supremacy over Manchuria; in Santo Domingo, Haiti, Mexico, Venezuela, Cuba, the Philippines, Samoa, Hawaii, Panama, Nicaragua, and China.

This shameless and, in the main, discreditable page of American history has been told of at length by Charles and Mary Beard in their monumental *The Rise of American Civilization.* Not only did profits from such enterprises keep those silent who might have protested against barbarities perpetrated within the United States by lynching mobs; such barbarities were contributed to and condoned by a theory of inferiority of darker peoples which grew out of and was contributed to by the needs of American and world imperialism. The two situations—internal and external alike—were and are closely interwoven. Thus what may at first seem to be developments which have no influence whatever upon lynching and the race problem generally within the United States becomes, in the light of world imperialism and the concentrated campaign of disparagement of coloured races, of both direct and indirect bearing upon the American race problem and the question of lynch-law.

All these diverse factors contributed, therefore, to an annual average of 166.5 lynchings between 1890 and 1900; to one of 92.1 between 1900 and 1910; to one of 84.0 in the decade following; and to one of 38.0 since 1920 and extending through 1927. Certain interesting changes are to be noted by examination of the annual averages between 1910 and 1920. It was during this decade that organized, intensive, intelligent, and persistent efforts against lynching were made for the first time. The sharp drop during this ten-year period and the seven years since is beyond all doubt due largely to the energetic efforts of the National Association for the Ad-

vancement of Colored People, organized in 1909 and
chartered in 1911, and to the Commission on Interracial
Co-operation, with headquarters in Atlanta, which was
organized after the war.

Largely through the work of these organizations and
the growing articulateness of the press in condemning
lynching, in which several Southern papers did notable
service, there was a slight decrease during the first half
of the second decade of the new century. In 1915 the
annual toll jumped sharply to 145, of which ninety-
nine were Negroes and forty-six white; among the latter, however, the total was affected materially by the
lynching of twenty-six Mexicans, hatred against whom
was accentuated by the campaign against Villa during
that year.

After an encouraging drop to fifty-four lynchings in
1917, there was a rise to sixty-seven in 1918, to eighty-
three in 1919, and to sixty-five, sixty-four, and sixty-one
in 1920, 1921, and 1922 respectively. Here again
economic factors motivated a set-back in the battle
against the hosts of Judge Lynch. The European war
shut off abruptly the flood of immigrants who for years
had amply supplied the demands for unskilled labour
to dig in the mines, tend the furnaces, and do the other
manifold tasks of American industrial plants. So acute
had the situation become that even had not these industries been swamped with orders for various supplies
for the warring nations, they would have been hard

put for labour to handle normal conditions. There came then, starting in 1916, one of the greatest internal migratory movements of history and certainly the greatest movement of huge masses of people within the history of the United States—the migration within a decade of nearly two million Negroes from the South. By the following year even those Southerners who had at first greeted the departure of Negroes with relief and joy as the eventual solution of the race problem became apprehensive concerning the immense economic loss to the South from hundreds of thousands of acres uncultivated because the labourers to cultivate them had fled. Resort was had to the old stand-by of a considerable majority of Southerners in dealing with Negroes—reliance upon terrorism and persuasion by brute force. Also, in addition to the passions let loose by war was one of particularly virulent effect in the South at this time—fear that Negro soldiers would not be so willing to submit to the old indignities when they returned from European battlefields.

Almost before the first Negro soldier left the United States to fight for his country, plans were set in motion to convince him when he returned that his war service and experience would not affect his own status after the war had ended. A broken-down itinerant Methodist preacher was instrumental in reviving the absurd ritual and uniform of the old Ku Klux Klan of infamous memory; later a shrewd "publicity man" crystallized the rather vague notions of the preacher by modern business methods into a huge and, for a time, compact body of illiberalism and mobbism. The far South tangibly demonstrated its gratitude to Negro soldiers for helping make the world safe for democracy by lynching ten of them, some in the uniform of the United States Army, during the year 1919; two of the ten were burned alive. Mississippi and Georgia mobs murdered three returned Negro soldiers each; in Arkansas two were lynched, in Alabama and Florida one each.

The year 1923 witnessed some abatement of the postwar brutality, and as well the results of the campaign against lynching, particularly among the more liberal element of the South, which was beginning to shake off the bondage of the Klan. No factor was of greater importance in causing a material decrease in the number of victims of mobs in 1923 than realization by the more intelligent South that mobbing Negroes was not the best method of retaining Negro labour. With a place of refuge to which he could flee, even the most tractable Negro who naïvely had believed that "the Southern white man is the best friend of the Negro" was leaving the South whenever a lynching or a Klan outrage of some other variety was staged near him. Enlightened selfishness led the South to renewed efforts to put down lynching and ensure a larger measure of immunity from attack to Negroes. Thus 1923 saw twenty-eight lynchings; in 1924 and 1925 there was a further drop to sixteen and eighteen respectively; in 1926 there was a sharp rise to thirty-four, and in 1927 the number went down again to twenty-one.

The potency of these forces was seen in the introduction in Congress of a federal anti-lynching bill which passed the lower House in 1922 and was defeated only by a Senate filibuster.

All through the tangled, many-angled problem of lynch-law there stands out in bolder relief than any other the economic factor in determining the rise and fall of the annual number of victims of lynching. Until there is a clearer and wider recognition of this fact and a refusal to permit deliberate misleading of public opinion through introduction of extraneous, untrue, and vicious statements for the purpose of obscuring the real issues involved, there is great likelihood that lynching will never be eliminated from American life. The attempt to use charges of rape as the real and only cause of lynching is an instance of American hypocrisy of the most vicious sort. With all its "colour bar" laws and its shameless exploitation of blacks in South Africa, Kenya Colony, and the West Indies, Great Britain has never yet descended to so low and vicious an expedient to justify its exploitation. Perhaps in time even the states of the far South will raise themselves to the point where hypocrisy at least will be eliminated from the list of its crimes against the Negro.

CHAPTER SIX

SCIENCE, NORDICISM, AND LYNCHING

HERBERT ADOLPHUS MILLER, Professor of Sociology at Ohio State University, delivered at Denver in 1925 a needed warning to those who are inclined too hastily to accept preliminary findings of workers in various branches of the sciences, results which, though often significant, are in reality but the first steps towards knowledge. His words were especially directed against those who, to reinforce preconceived notions of race, pompously utter dogmatic conclusions that are based on insufficient and often faulty laboratory findings. "There is also," said Professor Miller, "the appropriation of the scientific jargon by the totally unscientific who rationalize their prejudices and think that God intended it so because they can say it in scientific terms." [1]

Professor Miller added another warning of value: "Another popular tendency is to transfer emotional adherence from religion to science, and then to become

[1] "Science, Pseudo-Science and the Race Question, An Address Delivered by Herbert Adolphus Miller, Professor of Sociology, Ohio State University, Before the Sixteenth Annual Conference of the National Association for the Advancement of Colored People, June, 1925"; published in the *Crisis* (October 1925).

as orthodox and dogmatic as the most fundamentalist of religions. The scientist may be both bigoted and intolerant. There is this difference from religion, however, that the scientific method prevents staying long at one place, so that while scientists may be petty and narrow their total ultimate result is enlarging and constructive." [2]

There is no field in which scientists, both real and pseudo ones, have probed that reveals more clearly than the race problem the soundness of Professor Miller's observations and the need for his warnings. The Stoddards, McDougalls, Grants, and Brighams have utilized science to prove that God or Gobineau long ago made inferior all possessors of non-white skins. But promptly scientists and scholars worthy of the name, such as Mall and Pearl and Boas and Goldenweiser and Lowie, have exposed the falsity or the insufficiency of the evidence upon which the pseudo-scientists have based their "proof" of Negro inferiority.

Unfortunately for the United States, the vogue which such books as *The Rising Tide of Color Against White World-Supremacy* have had has done much towards the inculcation of prejudice and fear among those who would not consider joining such a movement as the Ku Klux Klan. There is the human propensity to believe those things that coincide with one's prejudices and interests, and the equally human inclination to disregard

[2] *Ibid.*

all evidence, however sound and unquestionable, which runs contrary to those prejudices and interests. Thus the Klan recruited the more rowdy element, and the Nordic movement those of slightly higher mental calibre—and between them profoundly influenced the already tense racial situation in the United States and added to the antagonisms from which such a phenomenon as lynchings arises. The lyncher, the Klansman, the Nordicist, the disfranchiser, the opponent of advancement of the Negro or other dark-skinned race, found in books such as Stoddard's comforting assurance of the fundamental soundness of their prejudices. "Scientific jargon" which they did not know was jargon assured them that the Negro is inferior and that it is therefore for the general good to "keep him in his place."

Speaking of theories of the relative ability of various races which are based on brain weights and conformations, Sir Arthur Keith, president of the British Association for the Advancement of Science, in a conversation in London in 1927, declared that he would not go to the biologist or the anthropologist, but to the social philosopher, in seeking an answer to the question of relative superiority or inferiority. "For what is superiority?" he asked. "For life in London I undoubtedly have advantages over the native of central Africa. But put us both down in his own land and it is doubtful if I could survive while he would. Who then can say whether he or I is superior? There is no possible way to determine absolutely what is superiority or who is superior to anybody else—it all depends on circumstances and opportunities."

The distinguished American biologist, Professor Raymond Pearl of Johns Hopkins University, expresses a similar point of view in a letter to the writer. "On the broad question of racial superiority and inferiority I have repeatedly in my writings urged caution. That various races are biologically different is an obvious fact, but to assert that one is superior or inferior to another at once gets one into deep water from a philosophical point of view, because it all depends upon who decided upon the yard-stick by which superiority shall be measured. Furthermore, equality of opportunity is something that, broadly speaking, never exists in the comparison of large racial groups. This has led me to take the position that discussion of the relative superiority or inferiority of races is a futile business. My reaction always is to urge people to talk about something else where there is perhaps some hope of arriving somewhere. It is a problem which is incapable of final resolution in terms of variables which do not involve fundamentally emotion, taste, and prejudices. And, as was long ago pointed out, it is no good discussing taste."

It is almost a tragic circumstance that such reasoned and temperate conclusions as these gain circulation at but a fraction of the speed of those which sow the seed of racial hatreds and antagonisms. It is also deplorable that especially in the United States prejudices flame into being, and with such hysterical venom that they all but overwhelm those who counsel sanity and scientific accuracy. Of all the ideas that cause race hatred there is probably none which has been so dangerous as Nordicism in its various forms and manifestations. Those who claim to belong to that rather vaguely defined class have, of course, contributed largely to civilization. The danger lies in the propensity to exaggeration, in claiming that every human being from the garden of Eden who accomplished anything was Nordic, and in asserting that nothing worth while has ever been done by a person who did not belong to this select group.

Those in the United States whose efforts have been of especial harm to the Negro and who, in one fashion or another, have helped to fertilize and perpetuate ideas of Negro inferiority can be divided roughly into four groups. At the lowest end of the scale is the Ku Klux Klan. Next are those who are slightly more erudite and respectable and by the margin of that superiority to the Klan more dangerous—Stoddard, McDougall, Grant, and others less well known, whose arguments are persuasive and *printed*. Then come the scientists like Robert Bennett Bean of the University of Virginia, who, backed by imposing pages of figures and bewildering charts, seek by brain weights and convolutions to establish the inferiority of the Negro brain, and, of course, the superiority of the white brain. Finally, there come those who have no patience with the Nordicists, who reject all their "proofs" and demonstrate their unsoundness, but who fall victim to some of the very same prejudices that afflict the Nordic doctrinaires. Into this class fall such men as Frank H. Hankins, Professor of Economics and Sociology at Smith College, whose *The Racial Basis of Civilization* so thoroughly riddles the exponents of Aryan or Nordic theories, from Gobineau and Chamberlain down to Stoddard.

The immense number of persons reached by the arguments of these various groups, and the effect which their theories have had on the race problem and the question of lynch-law, necessitates at least brief consideration of them. Of the Ku Klux Klan—the "extreme form of Protestant nationalism" Professor Siegfried terms it—little need be said here. Newspapers, magazines, and books have been filled with charges and counter charges regarding it. Internal dissension within the movement, the apprehension of some of its highest officials in crimes of moral turpitude, and the reaction of the saner if more sluggish elements of Americans have hastened the downfall of this movement and the disillusionment of its dupes. Deserted by the less unintelligent men who joined it, the Klan has fallen into the control of the lower type—the very criminal element

that the Klan asserted it was opposing—and we thus
have the lawless definitely organized for vengeance and
ruthless pursuit of their own ends.

The significance of such a movement is that the Klan
was, first, the direct-action expression of a most dangerous doctrine of superiority which many Americans
hold who are too respectable or too timid to translate
it into violent action; and, second, that the reign of
whippings, tarrings and featherings, lynchings, and
other outrages furnished a sorely needed if obvious
example for the United States of the manner in which
intolerance can spread. Just as the Klan was in post-
Civil-War days against the Negro, so primarily was the
post-World-War Klan designed to "handle" Negro soldiers returning from fighting for democracy in Europe.
It is to be questioned, however, if even that lesson was
sufficient to warn against the bigotry which seems to
thrive so rankly in the United States. "The critical
sense is not the most highly developed in America,"
says Professor Siegfried; and when the honest American views the growth of bureaucracy, the abridgment of
rights of free speech, free press, and free assembly,
the vast extent of intolerance and bigotry, and the willingness to engage in actual or potential lynching which
have developed so alarmingly within recent years in the
United States, he must accord at least shamed agree-
ment with Professor Siegfried's statement. Even of such
honest men there are but a few who realize that a con-

siderable portion of this intolerance is the direct result of the habit of lynching and bigotry which has been directed against the Negro. The Ku Klux Klan, therefore, is but a concrete example of the price that not only the South, but the entire country, is paying for lynching.

The Nordicists, under the fire of sound scientific criticism, are not far behind the Klan in being exposed and ridiculed. Also like the Klan, they have not been convinced of their absurdities, one fears, but are merely more discreet and less brazen in the parading of the virtues which they claim to possess exclusively. The ballyhoo experts of a blue-eyed, blond-haired, dolichocephalic superman are not as articulate as they were immediately after the end of the World War, but there is ample evidence that the seed sown did not fall upon barren ground.

It is a most revelatory experience to note how closely the Nordic propaganda has coincided with the eras of exploitation of coloured peoples by white nations. It was no accident that in the nineties the ideas of Gobineau should gain popularity simultaneously with the beginnings of modern imperialism. Nor was it by chance that the revived Klan and the popularity of books by Madison Grant and Lothrop Stoddard should grow simultaneously after the World War. One can easily understand how all of these movements had their roots firmly grounded in economic advantage. Fear—most of it imaginary—whipped up to the point of fury hatred first of the Negro, and later of Catholics, Jews, foreigners, and every other group which might conceivably endanger the position of those who imagined themselves to be of unmixed Nordic blood.

One wonders why those who revealed such fears seemed at the same time to be so lacking in common sense or confidence in their superiority. It would seem that, upon reflection, the fact would occur to the boasters that each human being possesses a total of 65,-534 ancestors within only fifteen generations—a mother and father, two grandmothers and two grandfathers, eight great-grandmothers and great-grandfathers, and so on through geometrical progression to the total given. If a generous estimate is allowed of thirty years to a generation, this means that so great a number of persons within a period of just 450 years have contributed to the blood-stream of each of us; and if Sir Arthur Keith is correct in his estimate that "man has the respectable antiquity of a million years," who can know what his "race" really is?

Such a humbling and self-evident fact seems not to have occurred to the majority of those who led the Nordic parade. In its various forms the doctrine of the superiority of the white, blond dolichocephalic added mightily in tenseness to an already over-tense racial situation. A bigoted, ruthless reign in the United States of fanatics sworn to persecution of all whom they did not like or approve—and Negroes were but one of the objects of that intolerance—was but narrowly averted and the danger of its recurrence is not yet past. It is not beyond belief that there may come the ironic situation of control of America by a Protestant, white, gentile, "Nordic" oligarchy, with ruthless suppression of all other elements—there was for a time apparent certainty that the United States was headed for that state. Perhaps then, if such states as Mississippi be examples of the result of such dominance, and only then will the United States fully comprehend the fruits of race pride and conceit and their inevitable accompaniments—the lawlessness and bigotry which find outlet in, among other ways, lynch-law.

Theories of Negro Inferiority

Closely allied with the efforts of the Klan and the Nordicists and playing a not unimportant part in the creation of a national psychology towards the Negro are the various attempts to prove Negro inferiority by brain weight or structure. From almost the beginning of the study of the human brain efforts have been made to prove that the brains of so-called inferior races—and, in the United States particularly, the brain of the Negro—are of a "simple and embryonic type." A. J. Parker in 1878 asserted and sought to prove that the Negro's brain bore an unmistakably closer relationship to that of the ape than to that of the white man, but his work was soon discredited by Tiedemann, Luschke, Marshall, and Mall who demonstrated that Parker was careless, superficial, scientifically incorrect, and animated by an obvious prejudice.

In 1906 Robert Bennett Bean of the University of Virginia published the results of a study which he had made of the brains of 103 Negroes and forty-nine whites taken from the bodies of derelicts unclaimed at death in the Baltimore morgue. The psychological approach of Bean to his study can best be learned from his statement that "there is less respect for the dead among Negroes" and that therefore the Negro brains examined were from the better class of Negroes, and their weights and measurements were fair averages for the entire race; while the white brains were from "only the lowest classes of whites . . . especially among the women, who are apt to be prostitutes." In a letter to the writer Professor Bean states that "the Negro brains were largely of the true Negro type of Central Africa and the Congo and West Coast, although some of them were undoubtedly of mixed origin, part white," which is, at best, a somewhat risky assertion when one considers the source of the bodies from which the brains were taken; while "the white brains were of the submerged tenth of the City of Baltimore."

It probably did not occur to Bean that the truth might be precisely the opposite of his generalization as to "less respect for the dead among Negroes" and the Negro brains' being a fair average for the race. Negroes are inclined to membership in burial societies or they carry insurance upon their lives to provide decent burial. Likewise there is a marked tendency towards charity among Negroes to save one of their own from burial in the potter's field, and especially from the dreaded dissecting-table.

But, leaving such considerations aside, Bean reported that "the average brain weight is greatest in the Caucasian male, least in the Negro female, and intermediate in the Negro male and the Caucasian female." [3] Dr. Franklin P. Mall of Johns Hopkins University, who had suggested that Bean make the study, was not satisfied with Bean's findings, and weighed and studied the brains himself. *"In order to exclude my own personal equation,"* he wrote later of his results, *"which is an item of considerable importance in a study like this,* all of the tracings as well as the measurements . . . were made *without my knowing the race or sex of any of the individuals from which the brains were taken.* The brains were identified from the laboratory records just before the results were tabulated." [4] (Italics ours.)

Dr. Mall found, *with the labels removed,* that Bean had overweighed the white brains and underweighed the Negro ones. In brief, the "personal equation" apparently played a considerable part, a clear example of

[3] "Some Racial Peculiarities of the Negro Brain," *American Journal of Anatomy,* Vol. V, No. 4, p. 386.
[4] *American Journal of Anatomy,* Vol. IX, No. 1.

Dr. Pearl's "it all depends upon who decided upon the yard-stick by which superiority shall be measured."

Dr. Mall reported in the *American Journal of Anatomy* the differences he found between the weights and measurements of Bean and his own. "My figures do not confirm Bean's result that the genu is relatively larger and the splenium relatively smaller in the white than in the Negro brain. The specimens I examined include 18 brains which Bean studied, and I find that the measurements I made of the areas of the genu and splenium in them do not agree altogether with his. . . . I think my chart shows conclusively, as far as possible with the method I employed, that there is no variation in either genu or splenium of the corpus callosum due to either race or sex. . . . I must therefore conclude that with the methods at our disposal it is impossible to detect a relative difference in the weight or size of the frontal lobe due to either race or sex, and that probably none exists. . . . The study has been still further complicated by the personal equation of the investigator. Arguments for difference due to race, sex and genius will henceforward need to be based upon new data, really scientifically treated and not on the older statements."

Not only has Mall's call for new data been answered, but much of that data has exploded various pet theories of the near-scientists, such as assumptions of correlation between brain weight and intelligence, between physical characters and intelligence, and between shape of head and mental agility. An amusing feature of the last named is the boast of the Nordics of dolichocephaly —and the fact that the Negro is the most dolichocephalous of races!

Of possible correlation between brain weight and intelligence Raymond Pearl concluded, basing his conclusions on five series of brain weightings representing Swedish, Hessian, Bavarian, Bohemian, and English sub-races of man and including altogether the weights of 2100 adult male and 1034 adult female brains, that "the degree of the correlation between brain-weight and intelligence is indeterminate, with the probability that it is sensibly equal to zero. That is, brain-weight and intelligence in the sense of mental capacity are probably not sensibly correlated. . . . There are definite racial types in brain-weight. The differences between racial groups in this character are only in part to be accounted for by differences in other characters of the body." [5]

Those who seek to find in the Negro's biological differences from the white evidence of mental inferiority will find little comfort in the study made by Karl Pearson, F. R. S., of head measurements of upwards of a thousand Cambridge graduates and of considerably more than five thousand schoolchildren. He concluded

[5] "Variation and Correlation in Brain Weight," *Biometrika,* Vol. IV, (June 1905–March 1906), pp. 80, 82.

that "the onus of proof that other measurements and more subtle psychical observations would lead to more definite results may . . . be left to those who *a priori* regard such an association as probable. Personally, the result of the present enquiry has convinced me that there is little relationship between the external physical and the psychical characters in man"; and he warns: "Let us hesitate on the ground of slender, or worse than slender, unscientific evidence to proclaim close association between intelligence and external physical measurements. So far there is nothing to encourage belief in such association; and if we are consistent and apply any of the dogmatic views currently held to the problem of interracial intelligence, we are led to very remarkable conclusions!" [6]

Nor have the scientists been any kinder to the Nordic's claims that his boasted dolichocephaly is the cause of superior intelligence. Dr. G. E. Harmon of the School of Medicine of Western Reserve University concluded, after studying 5600 males from Francis Galton's Second Anthropometric Laboratory Series, that "for males the degree of association between head breadth and head length and reaction time to both sight and sound in each instance is too small to be of any service for purposes of estimation. Or, as far as the mental element in reaction time is concerned . . . *the size and shape of the*

[6] *Biometrika,* Vol. V, (October 1906–June 1907), pp. 136, 128.

head have little if any association with the working of the brain." [7] (Italics ours.)

Dr. J. R. Musselman of Johns Hopkins University investigated the problem as to whether or not any relation can be found between head size or shape and mental agility, as represented by reaction times to sight and sound, studying 1850 individuals between the ages of three and seventy-six, and reached the same conclusions as Dr. Harmon. He reports: "As far as cephalic index is concerned . . . the correlation ratio is insignificant for both reaction times, or mental agility is not associated with either brachycephaly or dolichocephaly. . . . While there is a small amount of correlation between head breadth and reaction time to sound, its intensity is so slight as to be of no prognostic value." [8]

Let us return to Bean's effort to prove that Negro brains must be different from and inferior to white brains, for which, as has been seen, there is no scientific proof worthy of the name. The effect of Bean's study is perhaps most clearly seen in its effect upon so sound a scientist as Professor Frank H. Hankins of Smith College. In 1926 Hankins published his excellent *The Racial Basis of Civilization,* one of the most thorough,

[7] "On the Degree of Relationship Between Head Measurements and Reaction Time to Sight and Sound," *Biometrika.* Vol. XVIII (July 1926), p. 220.

[8] "On the Correlation of Head Measurements and Mental Agility. Women," *Biometrika,* Vol. XVIII (July 1926), p. 200-1.

painstaking, and informed expositions yet written of the fallacies upon which the Nordic doctrine is based. When, however, towards the end of his book, Hankins comes to a discussion of relative brain weight and conformation of white and Negro brains in a chapter entitled "Are Races Equal?" he accepts and quotes Bean as an authority—apparently unaware of Mall's exposure in 1906 of the bias and incorrectness of Bean's figures and conclusions. Hankins states: "Bean found that his negro brains showed a mode or center of greatest frequency between 1100 and 1200 grams while for his white brains the mode lay above 1300"; and later he reaches the conclusion that "it seems possible to say that there is no respect whatever in which white and negro are equal, —physically, intellectually or emotionally." [9]

In further substantiation of his conclusion Hankins quotes Spitzka's comparison in the matter of cranial capacity to the effect that "of 64 eminent men . . . the cranial capacity was 1650 cubic centimeters on an average, or 100 above the average for Parisians and 173 above that for negroes as given by Boule" [10]—regarding which Professor Pearl declares that "the Spitzka comparison is utterly meaningless and deserves no consideration whatever." One cannot escape the conviction that Hankins in his conclusions and in his acceptance of the discredited and worthless evidence of such men as

[9] *The Racial Basis of Civilization,* pp. 315, 323.
[10] *Ibid.,* p. 310.

Bean and Spitzka was either much influenced by "the personal equation" or did not know of the work of abler and less biased scientists than those upon whose work he relies.

Hankins's conclusions are all the more amazing in view of his statements regarding that question which so sorely agitates American minds—intermarriage. Hankins asserts unequivocally: "Even as regards white-negro crosses one can see no sound biological argument against them," since "the progeny, representing as they do a blend of ancestral characteristics, have their qualities determined not by some mysterious influence of race mixture, but rather by the genetic factors of their ancestors regardless of race." [11] But Bean, quoted and considered by Hankins as an authority, is convinced that "the tall, fair-skinned Negro (or mulatto), of the enterprising nature," is "the most dangerous of all characters to human society." [12]

Elsewhere Bean asserts that mulattos forming the bulk of the serving class in Virginia and North Carolina and who are descendants of Kaffir and Hamitic or Semitic crossings are "particularly noted for their height and intelligence, but are deceptive and dishonest, although they make good body-servants and house-servants"; that of three types of mulattos one is made up of those with all Negro features except colour; an-

[11] *Ibid.*, p. 347.
[12] *Op. cit.*, p. 399.

other, distinguished by "a peculiar mottling of the skin,"
is "inferior physically and mentally"; and the two
classes "represent one of the gravest menaces to society. . . . They seem to inherit all the bad of both
black and white." A third class of mulattos so nearly re-
sembles the Caucasian that "one has to look twice to be
sure"; but "they are almost invariably of a delicate
mold, and die young." Yet in the same article Bean, asserting that Negro brains are deficient, compared with
the white, in nerve-cells and nerve-fibres, declares that
"the possibilities of developing the negro are therefore
limited, *except by crossing with other races*"; that "having demonstrated that the negro and the Caucasian are
widely different in characteristics, due [*sic*] to a deficiency of gray matter and connecting fibers in the
negro brain . . . a deficiency that is hereditary and can
be altered only by intermarriage, we are forced to conclude that it is useless to try to elevate the negro by education or otherwise, except in the direction of his natural endowments"; and, finally, that "it is evident that
the brain of the American negro weighs more than the
native African, which is no doubt because of the greater
amount of white blood in the American negro." [13]

Here we have a bewildering example of much of the
reasoning on the alleged inferiority of the Negro—first,
the mulatto is "deceptive," "dishonest," "inferior physically and mentally," and "dangerous" and he "almost

[13] "The Negro Brain," *The Century*, Vol. LXXII, pp. 778–84.

invariably" dies young the nearer he approaches the Caucasian; and, second, the only hope of making anything at all of the poor Negro lies in intermarriage and crossing with other races! Such logic reminds one of the statement of a character in Somerset Maugham's *Of Human Bondage* who declared: "I thought it was only in revealed religion that a mistranslation improved the sense."

Nor is Hankins much less reluctant than Bean to give pontifical judgments that are both loose and inaccurate. He asserts that "under favorable circumstances few negro children finish high school work successfully, and fewer still complete a college course"—a statement which at best is a generalization in view of the large number of Negroes who each year are completing the courses of colleges and universities, to say nothing of high schools, facts which Hankins could have secured with very little effort. More, it is well known that these graduated, not under "favorable circumstances," but in the face of severe economic and other handicaps, such as, for many of them, the hostility of white fellow-students. Hankins also declares: "It may well be doubted whether there could be found any pure negroes who, if brought up under the most favoring circumstances, could develop the intellectual powers necessary to carry on the higher cultural activities of this country"—another loose generalization, incapable of proof in the face of prejudice which makes "favoring circumstances" for

Negroes almost coincidental with the millenium; and, like the statement about Negro graduates, a statement of which much can be presented in refutation, such as eminent Negroes with little if any white blood—Robert Russa Moton, Roland Hayes, Paul Robeson, Claude McKay, John Hurst, William Pickens, Paul Laurence Dunbar, Lucy Laney, Mary McLeod Bethune, George W. Carver, Robert S. Abbott, Eric Walrond, for example—and many others less famous. Here are black men and women of national fame and some of international reputation who in the arts, education, sciences, journalism, and administrative fields stand as refutation of Hankins's sweeping statement.

More attention has been given to such statements of Bean and Hankins than is deserved, when one takes into account the work of less biased scientists who have found results so much at variance with those of these two men. This has been done not because of their importance, but because they are more or less typical of a certain type of "scientific" thinking which has intensified the anti-Negro psychology so prevalent in the United States. Though remote, such reinforcement of prejudice plays a not insignificant part in making lynching, unequal educational and industrial opportunities, and other forms of race oppression possible.

It is certain that no conclusions regarding the Negro brain, whether those conclusions be absolute or relative, are worth very much until examination by unbiased and

competent scientists is made of a sufficiently large number of Negro brains. It is obviously most important that
such studies be made of the brains of Negroes who are
above the rank of criminals, prostitutes, paupers, mental
defectives, and other lower elements of the race. "We
have no good series of Negro brain weights," says Dr.
Pearl, "though we have several excellent series for
whites, but not for whites in America." Thus when it was
popular to base notions of racial ability upon brain
weights, before that theory was discredited, the brains of
men eminent in science, literature, and other fields demanding extraordinary ability and attainment, and of
students at universities such as Cambridge were weighed
—and from the results an average weight for the *white*
brain was secured. Against these a few hundred brains
of unknown and of the very lowest types of Negroes were
weighed—and the result determined the average for
all Negroes!

A severe blow was struck in 1928 at those who have
sought to prove inferiority or superiority by means of
relative brain weightings and conformations by Dr.
Henry H. Donaldson of the Wistar Institute of Anatomy
and Biology. Dr. Donaldson made, with the aid of Myr-
telle M. Canavan of the Wistar Institute, a study of the
brains of three eminent scholars—Dr. G. Stanley Hall,
Sir William Osler, and Edward Sylvester Morse. In
the *Journal of Comparative Neurology* for August 1928
(Vol. 46, No. 1) Dr. Donaldson reported that he had

been unable to find that the brains of these superior men differed markedly from those of ordinary men— "the brain, after death," he asserts, "is therefore but the crude machine lacking power and controls, and although the convolutions differ somewhat, yet, in view of the controlling numerical and quantitative conditions, variations in the convolutions can hardly be used to explain mental traits and abilities as between persons of ordinary and superior intelligence." As for the size of brains, "good growth yields not only a larger brain, but implies good nutritive conditions that favour functional activity," Dr. Donaldson concludes. As for nerve tissue, he declares that "unknown are the individual chemistry of the nerve tissue in each brain, the intimate connections between the neurons and the blood in all of its relations. These unknowns constitute the power and regulators for the brain as a machine."

In brief, it is Dr. Donaldson's conclusion after study of the brains of these three men of unusual ability that brain weightings, convolutions, and sizes mean very little in so far as they reveal superior or inferior mental ability in the light of present knowledge.

For whatever the results may be worth, it is to be hoped that the methodology of the past will be abandoned and not only that qualified and unprejudiced experts may study a sufficient number of Negro brains to make their findings valuable and trustworthy, but that, as with whites, such studies may take into consideration heredity, education, achievement, economic status, physical condition at time of death, and the myriad other factors which apparently determine so largely brain conformation. Such studies, replacing those of unknown Negroes, obviously would be the only ones which would offer a safe and fair basis for comparison with the studies of the brains of gifted whites.

Most of the old figures are precisely as valuable as would be a comparison of the brains of one hundred derelicts from London slums with those of an equal number of Indians of the type of Gandhi, Tagore, and men of like ability, with a conclusion based on such figures that Englishmen were hopelessly inferior. Or, to bring the hypothetical comparison even closer, to compare the brains of a given number of "Nordics" from the backwoods of Mississippi, Georgia, and Tennessee with those of a selected group of gifted Negroes such as W. E. B. Du Bois, James Weldon Johnson, Countee Cullen, Paul Robeson, George W. Carver, Mordecai W. Johnson, Ernest Everett Just, Roland Hayes, and Robert Russa Moton. Whatever its scientific value, such a comparison might at least offer opportunity for Gargantuan laughter.

Intelligence Tests

As biology and anthropology have been used to attempt to prove the physical inferiority of the Negro, so has psychology been turned, at times, to the same end.

"In the past decade," to quote Dr. Miller's Denver address again, "psychology has achieved an immense importance. It now talks as though it were grown up while it is still only a very vigorous adolescent." And nowhere does psychology speak with greater assurance than in the matter of so-called intelligence tests. It is certain that from such tests, fairly and intelligently applied, valuable hints as to the ability of the examined may be gained. Unfortunately, the American passion for regimentation and "efficiency" hampers the slow process of finding out exactly what can be learned from such tests. We are eager, once a few facts are in hand, to assume and to proclaim that the most minute reaction of the examined mentality is in our possession—especially if the few preliminary facts bear out ideas and prejudices we already possessed before the tests were made.

"Any conclusions drawn from the so-called intelligence tests," says Professor Pearl, "as to the relative intellectual status of individuals and groups are at best suggestive, and in no sense final"; and such an attitude is obviously the only safe and intelligent one to take. Otherwise too hasty conclusions cause, in some instances, discomfort and embarrassment. Such was the fate of Professor C. C. Brigham of Princeton, who sought to prove Negro inferiority by means of the results of the army mental tests. In his *Study of American Intelligence* Brigham proved, at least to his own satisfaction, that Negro draftees were of the average intelligence of a nine-year-old against an average of twelve years for whites. When confronted with the evidence that *Northern Negroes* were considerably superior to *Southern whites,* superior educational and economic advantages playing so important a role, Brigham demonstrated extraordinary agility in reaching the conclusion that such figures proved that the Negroes in question were "exceptions" and *must* have white blood.

Brigham's embarrassment was no less than that of the school authorities of a large Southern city, who, in accordance with modern ideas of education, engaged expert psychologists to test all pupils, white and black, in the public schools. To their dismay the tests proved the Negro children superior. It is hardly necessary to add that the results were promptly suppressed!

The danger of generalizations based upon such inquiries as in the army Binet test may best be seen by examining some of the problems presented in wholesale lots to the soldiers and upon which conclusions were confidently based by Brigham and others. A few of these tests are so patently absurd when applied to some of the individuals examined that the hasty reader might be inclined to dismiss all the tests without further thought. For example, pictures of a tennis-court without a net and of an electric light bulb with the centre filaments missing were placed before the subject, and his quickness in discovering what was missing was measured. The task obviously would be simple, for example, to a drafted man from, let us say, New York or Chicago, where tennis-courts and electric lights are not uncommon. Imagine, if you will, the plight of the draftee, white or Negro, from, let us suppose, rural Mississippi. Tennis-courts and electric illumination being much less common there than in a Northern city, he would of necessity take longer to name the missing parts, if he was able to do so at all. Confronted with a picture of a one-handled plough or a wickless oil lamp, he would probably, on the basis of that question alone, rate higher in perceptual ability than a New York or Chicago youth to whom a plough or an oil lamp would be relatively foreign.

Horace Mann Bond details the general attitude of some of those who "play the major indoor sport among psychologists" of testing Negro children. "If Negro children make lower scores than white (having already discounted the influence of social status), they are inferior, they were born that way and though we had a sneaking suspicion that this was the fact all along, we are now able to fortify our prejudices with a vast array of statistical tables, bewildering vistas of curves and ranges and distributions and the other cabalistic phrases with which we clothe the sacred profession of Psychology from the view of the profane public." [14] Bond, however, examined an unselected group of Negro children from professional, middle-class and labouring

[14] The *Crisis* (October 1927), Vol. XXXIV, No. 8, p. 257.

homes, keeping in mind environment as a possible factor instead of discounting it. He used with scrupulous attention the most approved testing and statistical technique and sometimes " 'leaned over backward' . . . in order to maintain 'scientific' accuracy." Bond used the original Binet-Simon test in the form revised by Professor Lewis Terman of Leland Stanford University. With approximate normality ranking as 100, Bond found that sixty-three per cent of the thirty children examined made scores of above 106 (according to Terman only thirty-three per cent of white children may be expected to make such a score); forty-seven per cent of the Negro children exceeded an I. Q. score of 122 (Terman states that only five per cent of white children may be expected to equal or exceed such a score); while forty-two per cent of the Negro children had an I. Q. of above 125, which score Terman estimates that only three per cent of white children may be expected to possess. More, twenty-six per cent of the Negro children rated above 130, a most select group, which Terman estimates not more than one per cent of whites reaches; and one Negro girl made the astounding figure of 142.

These remarkable findings are significant. Do they prove that Negro children are much superior to white? Not at all, though such a claim might have been made had Bond possessed the same general willingness to jump to conclusions and to deduce racial characteristics from individual tests which characterizes Brigham and his school. They simply indicate that it is a precarious business to generalize about racial mental ability.

Briefly, what is the nature and extent of the evidence to date upon which notions of racial mental differences and capacities are based? As long ago as 1910 R. L. Woodworth in an article appearing in *Science* disposed of the popular myth that so-called primitive races have greater acuity of sight, smell, or hearing when compared with civilized races, and of the corresponding notion that civilized peoples excelled in such other mental traits as reasoning power. "We are probably justified in inferring," he concluded, "from the results cited that the sensory and motor processes, and the elementary brain activities, the differing in degree from one individual to another, are about the same from one race to another."

So much for the psycho-physical tests. In the field of psychological tests many have worked and much has been published based upon that work. Careful and unbiased students, however, realize that there are so many elements which go into the making of the "racial mind," and the individual mind as well, that it is exceedingly unwise, if not dishonest, to lay down any broad and fast rules. In truth, only the outermost edges of this vast field have as yet been touched, though, to hear some of the experimenters speak, one might infer that nothing remained to be discovered. Some of these have ignored the economic status, the extent and quality of school facilities, the mental and cultural family backgrounds, the influence of prejudice and similar vital factors in shaping the mental attitudes and responses of Negroes examined. Then when some of these Negroes have been found to have a lower intelligence quotient, such deficiencies have promptly been termed proof of racial inferiority.

In addition to the army tests there have been some twenty or more studies on about 3500 Negro subjects ranging in age from five to thirty-five years of age. These include Strong and Morse's study of 125 Negro schoolchildren in Columbia, South Carolina, where the remarkable premise was laid down that the educational facilities of the white and coloured children were the same—which must have been surprising even to the school authorities of that Southern city. They found Negroes inferior to whites, but, in pursuing their inquiries, learned that the difference between city whites and mill whites was almost the same as that between Negroes and whites as a whole. The investigators promptly concluded that the mill whites were inferior *because of poorer social and economic advantages, but that the Negroes' lower rating was due to racial inferiority!*

In New Orleans 116 Negro and 112 white children of Irish, German, Italian, and French nationality of about the same economic and social circumstances as the Negro children were examined by D. Summe in

1917, using the Binet and Yorkes Point scales. Summe discovered that, on the whole, sex differences were much greater than the racial ones and that coloured girls made higher averages than the white boys. He also learned that the Negro children had a keener sense of observation, flatly contradicting Strong's and Morse's findings, in which they said they had found Negro children to be deficient in this respect.

Other studies have been made by Phillips in Philadelphia, Murdock in New York City, Pressey and Teter in Indiana, Odum in Philadelphia, Schwegler and Win in Kansas, Ferguson in Virginia, Willis Clark in Los Angeles, and a number of others. Goldstein studied and measured over three hundred coloured boys and girls and found that the differences between white boys and girls were greater than the difference between the coloured and white groups. Stetson gave memory tests to five hundred white and an equal number of Negro children in the fourth and fifth grades of Washington schools. On finding the coloured children lower in school studies he considered no other factors and assumed the inferiority to be due to deficient reasoning power. Pyle learned from a study made in three Missouri towns that Negro children approached the white norm in the same degree as their social and economic status.

Ferguson of Virginia tested 486 whites and 421 Negroes between the ages of nine and twenty-one. He gave four tests to determine extent of logical inference and reasoning or controlled association, comprehension of meaning, attention, perception, and discriminative reaction, and of motor co-ordination, speed, and accuracy. Although Ferguson did not discuss environmental differences, his results show that the whites excelled on mixed relations and completion tests, that coloured girls were superior to white boys in the cancellation tests, and that in the maze tests no racial differences were found. Of the four tests there was considerable overlapping and the two tests in which whites excelled were in fields distinctly influenced by formal education— and Ferguson did not go into the vast difference between the school facilities afforded by Virginia to its white and to its Negro children. Professor Robert E. Park of the University of Chicago severely criticized some of Ferguson's deductions and conclusions as to Negro inferiority, pointing out not only the notorious inferiority of schools provided by Southern states for coloured children, and the lower salaries paid Negro teachers, but that the economic handicaps of the Negro parents resulted in poorer food and, where the mother was forced to work, less home training.

The army studies constitute the largest array of data yet made. They reveal that the Southern Negro is as inferior to the Northern one as Negroes as a whole are to whites as a whole. Even more dismaying to those who seek to prove Negro mental inferiority is the revelation already noted which embarrassed Brigham of Princeton—that Northern Negroes are superior to Southern whites.

One of the most valuable series of psychological tests given to Negro and white children is that made by Willis W. Clark in Los Angeles in 1923. A summary of Mr. Clark's findings was given in the *Educational Research Bulletin* for November 12, 1923, published by the Los Angeles City Schools. Five hundred Negro children in five elementary schools were given certain mental and educational tests, and the results were compared with those obtained from the same tests given to the pupils of fifteen representative Los Angeles elementary schools. Comparison of the intelligence level revealed that "the median I. Q.'s and the distribution of intelligence over the various classificatory groups indicate that there is no significant difference shown in the intelligence level of the Negro children and that of children in the fifteen schools taken as a whole." The second test demonstrated that "the average accomplishment and range of accomplishment for Negro children are practically the same as for the total population of the fifteen schools."

Application of the Thorndike-McCall Reading Scale to test reading comprehension brought out that "the average ability for all Negro children tested was 0.203 of a grade below the norm, while that for pupils in forty elementary schools was 0.016 of a grade below norm. This is not a significant variation."

The Woody-McCall Fundamentals test of arithmetical ability revealed that "the average ability for all Negro children examined was 0.103 of a grade above the norm, while that for pupils in forty elementary schools was 0.38 of a grade above norm. The difference represents a little less than three months school work."

The Modified Ayres Spelling Test disclosed that the Negro children were 0.973 of a grade and white children in forty schools 0.79 of a grade below norm and that "although the Negro children are nearly a whole grade retarded in spelling ability, the situation is not materially different for the total school population."

In brief, such minor differences as were found would seem to suggest the possibility of the disparity being partly if not wholly attributable to differences in economic and other opportunities of the white and Negro children.

Only one thing can safely be determined from the tests made and material gathered to date on the intelligence of either whites or Negroes and that is that social status, economic circumstance, environment, racial and other prejudices (or lack of such prejudices), and a host of other factors enter into the equation with enormous weight. It is probable that whatever differences have been found between whites and Negroes are due to these factors far more than to any differences due to race if not entirely so. Such a conclusion seems well founded when one considers such studies as that made by Yerkes and Anderson of one thousand cases of whites, all of whose parents spoke English, from which study it was concluded that "difference in economic or social status can be correlated with different mental capacities, that difference being as much as thirty per cent." So with the study of city and country children, all of them white, which Pressey and Thomas made, where it was learned that the city children rated higher than country children and, more, that country children from the good farming districts were superior to those from poor ones.

As the technique of mental measurements is perfected, as means are found of eliminating the personal equation of the investigator himself in such studies, and as our present fragmentary knowledge of racial traits and psychology is enlarged, we may in time hope to determine what differences, if any, are due solely to race. Until that time has come, any conclusions are unwise at best, if not positively dangerous in the matter of race relations. Discrimination, injustice, brutality, and even lynchings are beyond all doubt due in part to the racial self-esteem of whites and their attitude towards those whom the pseudo-scientists have dubbed inferior, which has sprung from such false conclusions.

Summary

The data given in the preceding pages does not pretend by any means to present an exhaustive picture of scientific and near-scientific investigations of Negro mentality. Enough has been given, it is hoped, to indicate the nature of some of the best and some of the poorest inquiries into this difficult subject. It is also hoped that the reader may gain some idea of the way in which conclusions that at best are tentative have been used to increase prejudice against the Negro.

In the matter of the absolute and relative importance of brain convolutions it is certain that there is an insufficiency of accurate information about Negro brains, nor is there enough genuinely scientific data to justify sweeping statements as to Negro mental ability. A number of those who have made tentative investigations of the Negro brain and mental ability have been obviously animated by personal bias, and were willing and even eager to prove Negro inferiority by selecting the lowest types of Negroes for study and asserting the results thus obtained to be typical of the entire race.

There is danger in those who are thus willing to prostitute science for the purpose of affirming personal prejudices; but that danger is considerably lessened by those of genuine scientific mind who expose the meretricious work of the biased. While eventually the prejudiced and unscientific investigators will be discredited, the immediate danger lies in their giving the sanction of science to their prejudices, which in turn bear fruit in oppression and denial of opportunity, and, in a more remote fashion, help to keep alive a spirit of intolerance that finds expression in lynch-law. Such pseudo-scientists add to the too great amount of race hatred and race bitterness already in the world and work harm on all mankind by doing so.

Bernard Shaw, if memory be not at fault, once said that English oppression of Ireland could last only so long as Englishmen could think of the Irish as childlike, amusing, and inferior beings. So too can oppression of the Negro last only so long as ideas of his biological and mental inferiority persist, for it is largely upon such ideas that invidious distinctions are based.

The scientists who seek to rationalize their anti-Negro prejudices by commencing inquiries to find data which confirm their preconceived notions of racial superiority or inferiority and who jump too hastily to conclusions that are based on incorrect, inconclusive, or insufficient evidence are likely to involve themselves in embarrassing predicaments. There are biologists, evolutionists, psychologists, and anthropologists who assert that Negro traits as represented in mysterious chromosomes are always dominant in Negro-white crosses, while the so-called white traits are recessive, thus justifying their opposition to such crosses. If these notions are followed to their logical conclusion, it follows that "Nordic" or "Caucasian" stock, no matter how pure or how productive of eminent thinkers, scholars, explorers, colonists, and pioneers and superior men in all fields, always bows to the "inferior" Negro chromosome. If such an interpretation be correct, the western world's genius in developing means of rapid intercommunication between various parts of the world, the perfection of the telegraph and radio and automobile and flying-machine, would seem to foretell the equally rapid conquering of the "Nordic" chromosome—a destruction of the "superior" man by means of his own "superiority."

An interesting sidelight on the influence of other interests upon science was discovered when certain documents were sought in the library at Oxford University. It was found that the needed material could not be obtained because the files of certain American scientific journals were not in that library. Considerably more than half of the efforts to prove the inferiority of the Negro brain have been made by Americans; and, to the credit of American scientists, most of the sound work to disprove the assertions of biased men of science has also been done by Americans.

———

W HAT have lynchings cost the states which most frequently have practised them and what has been the price which they have exacted from the country as a whole? The disesteem in which the United States is held because of lynch-law is world-wide. Newspapers in Europe, South America, Canada, China, and Japan, and even in Africa report with astonishing regularity burnings, ordinary lynchings, and race riots in the United States. Such news items create in other countries emotions towards the United States which run the gamut from ironical laughter at American pronouncements of decency and fair play in world affairs to amazement and indignation that a so-called civilized country permits such unrestrained barbarity.

Throughout America as a whole lynchings by their very drama and news value have coloured, distorted, and poisoned thought upon the race question. They have helped to feed the flames of mobbism, which have found expression in terrible race riots in both North and South within recent years.

The effect of lynch-law is naturally most clearly seen upon those states where both the greatest number of lynchings have taken place and where lynching as an institution has been continued with little variation over a long period—which is to say, the South. Some of the deleterious effects have already been noted in preceding chapters—the irremediable harm done to the minds of children, the dominance of a narrow-minded and ignorant clergy, the distorting and magnifying of the sex factor. No claim is made, of course, that all these and the things about to be mentioned are due entirely to lynching or even to the race question as a whole. It cannot be denied, however, that a major share of the South's backwardness is due to the amount of effort it has put forth to keep the Negro down, and of all these efforts lynching, both in itself and as a symbol, takes first rank. Corrupt politics, a venal press, a bigoted clergy, impoverished minds, and a multitude of other evils could have been to a great extent averted had the energy which the South has devoted to keeping the Negro "in his place" been devoted to efforts towards enlightenment.

In 1925, when the newspapers of the entire world were filled with news of the tragi-comedy then being enacted at Dayton, Tennessee, in the trial of an obscure school-teacher for mentioning the facts of evolution to his pupils, even Americans were amazed that such a scene was possible in a supposedly enlightened age. To those who knew the South, and particularly the rural South, not only was there no surprise at such a spectacle, but Dayton fitted very snugly into its frame. Of all the factors which went into the making of the ignorance from which the scene sprang, none was so important as the South's attitude on the Negro.

For more than three hundred years those who sought to maintain slavery and those who in more recent times have defended lynching and other measures aimed against the Negro found it necessary to suppress ruthlessly all opinion at variance with their own. The more the pressure, first against slavery and then against lynching, the more necessary was deemed the crushing of objections, North and South, to the mass determination to suppress the Negro. This intolerance and bigotry, with measles-like propensity, inevitably spread to other controversial subjects. Little by little over a period of three centuries grew the demand, backed by the rope and the faggot, for rigid conformity on all controversial matters. Religion, politics, science, economic systems, education, moral codes—one by one the thinkers of the South on these and other aspects of life concerning which there always have been and always will be varying opinions found themselves beaten into submission and uniformity. Those who nurtured opinions or ideas contrary to the mass opinions and ideas of the South found it expedient either to remain silent or to get out of the South.

Health-giving dissent, without which neither a society or an individual can live and progress, died below the

Potomac. A vast and arid region, in whose ranks until very recent years there was no hint of revolt, spread itself before the eye of the observer. From this deadening regimentation there sprang quite naturally and luxuriantly such movements as the Klan, intolerant fundamentalism, blatant and ignorant politicians, a sterile artistic life and other logical fruits of too binding orthodoxy.

Against such a background Dayton, J. Thomas Heflin, Cole Blease, the Rev. J. Frank Norris, the Ku Klux Klan, the Bible Crusaders, astounding illiteracy, impoverished farms, and a host of other evils are easily accounted for. In *The Autobiography of an Ex-Coloured Man* James Weldon Johnson speaks of "the tremendous struggle which is going on between the races in the South" and makes this wise observation: "Though the white man of the South may be too proud to admit it, he is, nevertheless, using in the contest his best energies; he is devoting to it the greater part of his thought and much of his endeavour. The South today stands panting and almost breathless from its exertions." Elsewhere one of his characters remarks that "if the Negro is so distinctly inferior, it is a strange thing to me that it takes such tremendous effort on the part of the white man to make him realize it, and to keep him in the same place into which inferior men naturally fall."

The thought of meeting argument and reason always with force, which finds its seeds in lynch-law, permeates all phases of Southern thought. This was seen clearly in the anti-evolution fight, where such phrases were common, to take a typical utterance, as was used by a correspondent of the liberal Greensboro, North Carolina, *Daily News:* "Take the evolutionists, infidels, and no-hell teachers out somewhere and crucify them, head downward, and we will have a better country to live in"—though one would imagine that many Southerners, considering the lynchings and other enormities for which the South is responsible, would welcome a "no-hell teacher" with a sigh of relief. It is in such an atmosphere that a minister thrives who is of the type of the Rev. J. Frank Norris of Texas, indicted at various times for such pecadillos as arson and murder, and that an enthusiastic audience is given to statements such as "So help me God, I will not be a party to wink at, support, or even remain silent when any group, clique, crowd or machine undertakes to ram down the throats of Southern Baptists that hell-born, Bible-destroying, deity-of-Christ-denying, German rationalism known as evolution." [1]

Such idiotic appeals to mob psychology are typical of a certain type of Southerner and bear evidence of the state of mental decay with which the South is cursed. Fortunately for that section of the country the very violence and exaggeration of the Norris type create an-

[1] Quoted from *The War on Modern Science*, pp. 171–2, by Maynard Shipley (New York, 1927).

tagonism and help spur interest in and sympathy with the very objects of their denunciation—precisely as the anti-Negro tirades of Blease and Vardaman and their class create in the minds of genuinely intelligent persons a serious doubt of the soundness of the assertions of the Negrophobes. The Messianic delusions of Southern churchmen such as Bishop Candler of the Methodist Episcopal Church, South, that "the churches of the South will be lost"; the paradox of the Klan fighting, so it claims, for "separation of church and state," while its blood brothers, the Fundamentalists, are struggling for Church domination of the State through such measures as dictation of legislation banning the teaching of the doctrine of evolution, compulsory reading of the Bible in State-supported schools, and, in brief, putting "God into the Constitution"; interference with and crippling of universities and colleges which are struggling to bring some light into Southern darkness; persecution of individuals who are too intelligent to bow to the ideas and phobias and superstitions of the mob—all these handicaps that afflict the South, which at first seem far removed from the race problem and lynching, are found upon examination to be sprung from the same intolerance and mob domination that has characterized the South's treatment of the Negro for three centuries. This is one item of the bill which the lynching states are paying and must pay for unrestrained mobbism and intolerance.

Another striking paradox of the Southern situation, and a significant item in the price of lynching, is the attitude towards women. No boast is more frequently or vehemently made below the Mason and Dixon line than that women are nowhere more worshipped, enshrined, respected, or protected than in the South. So frequently have such statements been reiterated that even in the North many people hold the notion that Southern women belong to a peculiar class, different from and superior to women in any other part of the world. The truth lies between this pleasant myth and the sweeping indictment of white women of the South of the Rev. Mr. Owens of North Carolina to the effect that "there is the greatest possible danger . . . that in the future it may come to pass that you will send your daughter to the North for culture and she will come back with a little Negro." There are many persons, including some who are Northerners and some who are not white, who do not agree with the Rev. Mr. Owens and who believe that there are many Southern women who can be trusted away from the South. And as for the conception of Southern women as of a peculiar mould, another Southerner, William J. Robertson, in *The Changing South* strikes a powerful blow at the notion of any peculiar difference between the women of the South and any other part of the country or the world. He writes: "The automobile has brought unfavorable developments to the South just as it has to other sections of America. Joy rides are not infrequent, and have disastrous effects. Girls from the best families partici- pate in these adventures, the principal features of which are petting, using the contents of hip flasks and pa- tronizing roadhouses. . . ." And, in writing of "The 'Bible Belt,'" Robertson says: "'Them damn North- erners think they are smart,' a Southerner in nearly any rural section in the South will say as he goes about making his moonshine, seducing his neighbor's daugh- ter, going off with his neighbor's wife or committing murder, arson or assault and battery as the case may be."

It is not what the romanticists or John Powell or the Rev. Mr. Owens or William J. Robertson say concern- ing women which concerns us here, but the use to which the partly true, partly mythical exaltation of women —*white women*—in the South has been put. Being deposited upon a pedestal may be temporarily pleas- ant and even thrilling, but it loses much of its glamour for intelligent women when the elevation means denial of all rights save those of housework and child-bearing. Economic dependence, contacts with none save "po- lite, refined, womanly" pursuits, mental activities in no other field than home life—all these man-imposed re- strictions have borne more heavily upon women in the South, and have been maintained more rigidly, than in any other part of the country. Nowhere else has the "unwritten law" been invoked so frequently or successfully—upon the theory that once a woman through marriage has been "bought and paid for," she is a chattel of her husband and owner precisely as a Negro slave was before the Civil War. In protection of tangible possessions the right is reserved to the owner—so the theory in effect runs—to use physical force to resist encroachment upon his property, regardless of the wishes of the woman involved.

Stories of Negro propensities towards rape were utilized even further to restrict human desires of women of brain and ability to break away from "respect and chivalry," which, they learned, were not sufficient reward for denial of rights they possessed as individuals. In striking contrast with the showing of states where women were not blocked so much in efforts towards achievement is the record of women of the South listed in *Who's Who in America.* Her mind and activities bound for three hundred years, much as were the feet of Chinese women, it is only to be expected that in *Who's Who* so large a percentage of women from the South *who have remained in the South* are able to point only to literary efforts unknown beyond their own communities or to activities as prohibition workers or club presidents. As was seen in the letter quoted in the chapter on religion, a most promising revolt has begun to make its appearance among the more intelligent and progressive white women of the South against this system. Industrialization of the South will bring, undoubtedly, certain changes which are not for the best. But there are to be seen other changes which, causing women of the South to demand less cotton-wool "chivalry" and more recognition as individuals, will help not only themselves, but the South, to emancipation from the bungling of the past.

William H. Skaggs of Alabama in *The Southern Oligarchy* shows a phase of this attitude towards women: "Eight of the States that refused to ratify the amendment for equal suffrage are among the eleven that make up the Solid South. Arkansas, Texas and Tennessee are the three States in the South that ratified the amendment. The eight Southern States which refused to ratify the suffrage amendment are those which have the highest criminal record and the highest percentage of illiteracy. . . . Opposition in the South to prohibiting discrimination on account of sex . . . was based on the old political claptrap of the Southern Oligarchy —the alleged fear of Negro domination. 'It is for the protection of our mothers, sisters, wives and daughters that we oppose this measure,' said some of the political leaders of the South. This is the absurd propaganda that is always started in the South when the Oligarchy becomes alarmed about some measure providing for better educational opportunities, social or civic advancement, or other wholesome measures which would improve the condition of the people. . . ."

As poor whites were enslaved in reality along with

Negroes, so have white women been oppressed with Negroes. Realization of this obvious fact lends great significance to the statement of the Southerner quoted in the chapter on religion to the effect that "the most hopeful element in the church situation is the fact that women are coming into a larger . . . place in the life of the church," which applies to other phases than church life. White women of the South have been made to pay a tremendous price for lynching, but, to quote the same man again, "having recently come through their struggle for representation and self-expression, are very sensitive to any situation that denies this to others. . . ." Though white Southern women, and, even more, coloured women of the South, have been forced to bear a staggering part of the burden of mob bestiality and proscription which lynching and the race problem in general have exacted, there is little doubt that they in turn offer one of the most hopeful signs of a more enlightened and a more humane South.

Nor are these the only paradoxes the Southern scene presents. There is the boast of superiority of the lynching states—and the constant apologizing for the ills of the South. Preserver of Anglo-Saxonism, defender of the faith, and sole surviving champion of "real" religion, self (but eternally) -appointed guardian of the "purity of the white race," apogee of perfection! One would imagine that a section so abundantly gifted could

and would conquer any obstacle, no matter how in-
surmountable. Instead, speak of Southern shortcomings,
and what does one hear in reply?—that backwardness is
due to the Negro, the boll-weevil, poverty, carpet-bag-
gers, Northern viciousness and decadence, too much
rain, too little rain, the Civil War, evolutionists, no-hell
religionists—the list is endless. Burdens enough the
South has had, there can be no denying. But the self-
pitying, defensive attitude, which has so long sat somewhat strangely upon a self-admittedly superior race, has
done more to keep the South in its low position than all
its problems combined. Howard Odum, the brilliant and
courageous professor of sociology at the University of
North Carolina, summed up this fault in an address at
Emory University in 1924:

> We do not know enough.
> We do not think enough or well enough.
> We do not read enough or well enough.
> We do not write enough or well enough.
> We do not DO enough or well enough.
> We do not work together well enough, and
> We talk too much.

This Southern contradictory attitude of boasting and
whining springs, obviously, from the circumstance
mentioned in the chapter of "The Mind of the Lyncher."
Three hundred years of defence of the indefensible,
first of slavery and then of lynching and proscription,

could hardly have produced any other result. Boasting
to convince themselves and others of their superiority;
apologizing and shifting the blame for the failure of
accomplishments to coincide with the virtues claimed.

Another heritage of slavery and lynching is the idea
of labour's being discreditable, even dishonourable.
From this notion spring many of the ills especially of
the poor white, who in his ignorance furnishes a fertile
field for Ku Klux organizers, venders of worthless pat-
ent medicines, Fundamentalist evangelists of the Frank
Norris type, politicians of the Vardaman and Cole
Blease variety, and mob leaders. It leads to the lack of
success in organizing workers in the Southern states
and uniting the two groups, poor whites and Negroes,
whose interests are most closely interwoven. Race hostility, cleverly worked upon by means of stories of rape
and other tales of the sort, are used to perpetuate long
hours, low wages, and highly unsatisfactory conditions
for white and black labour alike. DuBois, in *The Negro,* tells of the beginnings of this cleavage of interests
shortly after the Civil War through the passage of labour laws "making the exploitation of Negro labor
more secure. All this legislation had to be accomplished
in the face of the labor movement throughout the
world, and particularly in the South, where it was beginning to enter among the white workers. This was
accomplished easily, however, by an appeal to race
prejudice. No method of inflaming the darkest passions

of men was unused. The lynching mob was given its glut of blood and egged on by purposely exaggerated and often wholly invented tales of crime on the part of perhaps the most peaceful and sweet-tempered race the world has ever known. Under the flame of this outward noise went the more subtle and dangerous work. . . . Labor laws were so arranged that imprisonment for debt was possible and leaving an employer could be made a penitentiary offense. . . . The acquiescence of the white labor vote of the South was further insured by throwing white and black laborers, so far as possible, into rival competing groups and making each feel that the one was the cause of the other's troubles." [2] In the forging of chains for the hands of black workers, white workers bound their own limbs and it will be many years before those shackles are finally broken. Again, the rope and faggot, premier emblems of prejudice, served to entrench profits behind an almost impregnable wall, while those who helped construct the fortifications did not even suspect, prejudice being so potent an anodyne, the nature of the building they were erecting.

In two other fields the lyncher served to increase ignorance and prejudice—politics and the press. There are many who think of these two fields as major ones in the problem of race. In reality they are symptoms

[2] DuBois, *The Negro*, pp. 225-6.

more than causes and, like the Church, follow instead of leading.

From the framing of the Constitution to the Civil War, especially between 1830 and 1860, Southern politicians and office-holders were the puppets of the slavocracy and did their bidding when high tariffs or abolition or any other step inimical to the selfish interests of the slave-holders threatened. "Nor can it be truthfully said," Charles and Mary Beard write, "as southern writers were fond of having it, that a tender and consistent regard for the rights of states and for a strict construction of the Constitution was the prime element in the dispute [over slavery] that long divided the country. As a matter of record, from the foundation of the republic, all factions were for high nationalism or low provincialism upon occasion according to their desires at the moment. . . . Less than twenty years after South Carolina prepared to resist by arms federal officers engaged in collecting customs duties, the champions of slavery and states' rights greeted with applause a fugitive slave law which flouted the precious limitations prescribed in the first ten Amendments to the Constitution—a law which provided for the use of all the powers of the national government to assist masters in getting possession of their elusive property—which denied the alleged slave, who might perchance be a freeman in spite of his colour, the right to have a jury trial or even to testify in his own behalf. In other words, it was 'con-

stitutional' to employ the engines of the federal authority in catching slaves wherever they might be found
in any northern community and to ignore utterly the
elementary safeguards of liberty plainly and specifically
imposed on Congress by language that admitted of no
double interpretation." [3]

This attitude of selfishness has continued to charac-
terize the positions taken by Southern "statesmen" in
Congress and in national affairs to this day. It gives
them the palm without question, for inconsistency and
selfishness are the rule instead of the exception. Southern members of both houses of Congress engage in lusty
battles for federal aid in flood relief, for prohibition,
and anti-evolution laws, and do not hesitate to demand
tariff protection of cotton, sugar, and other products of
the South while as loudly demanding free trade on non-
Southern products. The same members will orate and
filibuster until blue in the face for the "preservation
of states' rights," against federal interference in industries such as child-labour and lynching—uttering
sonorous and windy orations against such "interference"
with convenient forgetfulness of their pleas for federal
action when such action happens to give aid to Southern
projects.

Fear—abject fear—of "Negro domination," against
which the rope and the faggot still stand as emblems,

[3] Charles and Mary Beard, *The Rise of American Civilization*, Vol.
II, pp. 40–1.

have led to political sterility and the election to office
from the Southern states of men who, with practically
no exceptions, rank little above petty village politicians. Walter Hines Page some years ago summed up in
a few words the effect of this fear in an address before
the North Carolina Society of New York: "The South,
therefore, neither contributes to the Nation's political
thought and influence nor receives stimulation from the
Nation's thought and influence. Its real patriotism counts
for nothing—is smothered dumb under party systems
that have become crimes against the character and the
intelligence of the people."

The foisting of inferior and demagogic mountebanks
upon the country by the South found its counterpart in
journalism in the South, though, fortunately, the press,
in inspiring contrast with the politicians, is showing
signs of emergence from the doldrums of ignorance and
prejudice. The time is not long past when hardly a newspaper of the South dared speak even faintly against
lynching and many of them openly defended the practice. There still are journals today, especially in the
rural sections of the states in the far South, which will
not condemn the practice and deem it sufficient answer
to criticism of lynching from outside sources to point
to crime in Northern communities. But only the more
blatant dare openly defend mob-law and they do so on
the old ground of "protecting womanhood." In the suc-

ceeding chapter will be given some instances of the
change that is coming over the Southern press.

In the preceding pages are given a few of the more
important effects of the backwardness which mob-law
and mob psychology have caused in those states where
they have been most prevalent. While other factors have
shared responsibility for these deplorable conditions,
there can be little doubt that the lyncher's rope has both
directly and indirectly played the leading role in bringing such conditions into being. When these states
emancipate themselves from the rule of the mob, they
will not be saving the Negro and the occasional white
victim of the lyncher nearly so much as they will be
saving themselves. They are like Maria Insull in *The
Old Wives' Tale;* "superstitions and prejudices, deep
and violent, served her for ideas . . . benighted and
spiritually dead, she existed by habit." The South could
never have become the eternally dominant section its
orators extravagantly claimed it to be because of
geographic and economic conditions. Handicapped further by its own phobias, extending over a period of three
hundred years, it can hardly attain within a considerable number of years even the approximate progress and
intelligence of other sections of the country where many
minds and races have contributed their share, in contrast with the deadening Anglo-Saxonism of the South.
The price it has had to pay for its unrestrained brutality has been a heavy one and the end is not yet in

sight. One thing is evident. Whatever the South hoped to gain from its attitude towards the Negro, the price it has paid is far greater than that hoped-for gain; and, ironically, the South has failed to receive almost every one of the selfish benefits which it sought.

CHAPTER EIGHT

THE CHANGING SCENE

I T IS with relief that one is able to turn to indications of betterment of the conditions portrayed in preceding chapters. For many reasons pointing out the faults of the South has been a popular sport—largely because the task is made easy by the gigantic proportions of these shortcomings and the clearness with which they manifest themselves. The more complex a society, the more difficult it is to isolate even in broad outlines the forces which work within that society for good or evil. The South offers to analysts of social conditions a more primitive and thus a more simple panorama for examination. It is always easier to find out what makes the wheels go round in a Thomas Heflin than in a Thomas Edison.

There is no better method by which one can see the changes that are going on in the South—changes that are sometimes so slow as to be almost imperceptible—than by comparing the general attitude, as reflected in the press, towards two lynchings, fifteen years apart. More, both examples of lawlessness occurred within the state of South Carolina, in many respects to be classed with the more hopeless states, Mississippi, Florida, Georgia, and Arkansas.

In 1911 a Negro by the name of Willis Jackson, accused of attacking a white girl, was lynched near Greenville and his fingers were cut off and distributed as souvenirs. Joshua W. Ashleigh, a member of the South Carolina legislature, led the mob, which numbered among its members some of the most prominent men of the community. Ashleigh's son, editor of the *Intelligencer*, the local paper, assisted his father in leading the mob and afterwards made capital of the murder by issuing a special edition, in which he declared: "*The Intelligencer* man went out to see the fun without the least objection to being a party to help lynch the brute." Cole Blease was Governor at the time. He refused to use any of the power of his office to punish the lynchers, declaring his willingness to leave the governor's chair and help in a lynching when a Negro was accused of rape.

In 1926 a mob at Aiken, with the connivance and aid of officers of the law, took a woman, her younger brother, and her seventeen-year-old cousin and lynched them. The then Governor did nothing, though he was supplied with affidavits naming certain members of the mob. His successor evinced a greater keenness in checking Sunday golf-playing than in checking lynching. Cole Blease, elevated in the interim to the United States Senate, ran true to form by playing to the galleries, offering to defend any man indicted for the lynching

as soon as it was known that evidence had been gathered which implicated individuals in the mob.

At first glance the 1926 lynchings seem worse than
the one in 1911. The great contrast lay in the attitude
of the press. Led by the militant R. Charlton Wright
of the Columbia *Record,* other South Carolina papers
of the better type, such as the Columbia *State* and the
Charleston *News and Courier,* united in an uncompromising demand for the apprehension and punishment of the lynchers. When investigation by the
National Association for the Advancement of Colored
People was followed by a thirty-day featuring on the
front page of the New York *World* of the stories of a
special correspondent, the three South Carolina papers
mentioned renewed their demand for arrest of the
known lynchers. The *Record* scored mercilessly the
typically cheap gesture of Cole Blease, indicating that
he does not represent all the people of South Carolina.
Though failing to bring indictments and trials, the Aiken
case, through the efforts of the press of the state and
country, stirred South Carolina and the South as have
few similar events.

Back of this changed attitude, in which the lyncher
finds himself less popular and comfortable with each
passing year, lie a number of forces and the work of
several organizations. Some of the latter have directly
attacked the problems of lynching and the race question

generally; others, with no special thought of the Negro or of lynching, have helped bring about changes that have materially influenced both thought and action on this grave question. It is impossible here to do more than give a brief survey of the more important forces at work. An effort is made simply to indicate those that seem to be causing most of the changes.

One of the most notable of these changes, the causes of which will be noted shortly, is that already referred to—the white press. The great majority of Southern newspapers are still many leagues removed from advocacy of full participation of the Negro in Southern life, and particularly in the use of the ballot. Yet, measured by the attitude of but a few years ago, encouraging progress can be seen. Then practically every paper in the South, and many northern ones as well, featured his race in flaming headlines whenever a crime was charged to a Negro; then, as compared with the vigorous and unqualified condemnation of lynch-law today, journals that dared oppose lynching were almost unknown. Today hardly any paper of the South, save in the most benighted and rural sections, will openly defend lynching for any cause whatever.

The most notable instance of courage in the new press of the South is the Columbus, Georgia, *Enquirer-Sun*. Edited by Julian Harris, son of the late Joel Chandler Harris, and his brilliant wife, Julia Collier Harris, this journal in the face of advertisers' boycotts, loss of great percentages of their readers, and other financial difficulties, to say nothing of actual threats against their lives, has militantly and brilliantly fought lynching, the Ku Klux Klan, the anti-evolutionists, and every other emblem or manifestation of racial or intellectual bigotry. It fought the Klan when that movement absolutely dominated the state of Georgia and when even the Governor was a Klansman.

If there are no others of the calibre of the *Enquirer-Sun,* the number of papers that have repeatedly taken an unqualified stand against lynching is significant and growing. Among these are the Atlanta, Georgia, *Constitution,* the Columbia, South Carolina, *Record,* and *The State* of the same city, the Charleston, South Carolina, *News and Courier,* the Greensboro, North Carolina, *Daily News,* the Chattanooga, Tennessee, *Times,* the Birmingham, Alabama, *News,* the Houston, Texas, *Post,* the San Antonio, Texas, *Express,* and perhaps half a dozen others.

Of immense importance in helping to shape both white and Negro public opinion has been the growth of a considerable number of Negro newspapers and magazines. These range from inferior, cheaply printed local sheets of four pages to great national weeklies. The circulations of a few of these run as high as from fifty thousand to two hundred thousand. Most of the larger ones and many of the smaller are well edited. These papers exert an influence in the moulding of Negro opinion little realized by the white public. For Negroes have learned to read with considerable caution accounts in the white press of events involving white and coloured individuals. They go to their own press for such information. If these accounts are often as biased on one side as the press they distrust is on the other, they are no less potent in shaping Negro thought.

Especially united have these papers been on the subject of mob violence. They may differ on politics or religion, but on lynching and mob violence there is no division. In the prominence given stories of lynching, as well as in their editorial comment, the most unremitting emphasis on and opposition to mobbism is voiced continually in two hundred and fifty Negro newspapers against Judge Lynch. This terrific bombardment has helped create a stupendous racial consciousness on the question of lynching which has added mightily to the grim determination of Negroes to fight against moblaw. The Negro press has been of especial aid to such a movement as the National Association for the Advancement of Colored People.

Three monthly magazines, *The Crisis, Opportunity,* and *The Messenger,* exert an extraordinary influence on Negro opinion. The first named is the official organ of The National Association for the Advancement of Colored People; the second occupies the same relation to the National Urban League. All three are well written and frequently brilliant in their analyses of the underlying motives of race conflict or racial amity. They serve, with the Negro newspapers, to stiffen Negro resistance to oppression, to educate and develop a racial consciousness, and to inculcate pride in Negro achievement. In so doing they have notably changed and widened the scope of Negro thought and made it less wise and safe to attack Negroes.

Likewise of considerable importance have been the editorials of papers neither Southern nor Negro—the Northern white press, and notably the New York *World* —in opposition to and exposure of the details of lynchings. While most of the great metropolitan dailies have consistently written against lynching on the occasion of outbreaks, the *World* has a number of times, as in the Aiken triple lynching of 1926, sent correspondents to the scene, questioned the officials and editors of the state, and in other ways helped to focus public attention upon the problem.

Among the magazines *The Nation*, edited by Oswald Garrison Villard, has stood head and shoulders above its fellow journals and, in truth, above any other white publication of the United States in opening its columns to the facts and in editorial condemnation of mob violence.

Of the organizations that have laboured directly against lynching two stand out pre-eminently for the effectiveness of their work.

The most persistent, systematic, and organized attack upon lynching has been waged by the National Association for the Advancement of Colored People. This movement was organized in 1909 immediately after a disastrous race riot in Lincoln's old home, Springfield, Illinois, had given tragic emphasis to the growing seriousness of the race problem and the lack of organized effort towards lessening of friction between the races. The movement has its national headquarters in New York City and upwards of four hundred branches in all parts of the United States. It numbers among its national officers, board of directors, and branch officers some of the most distinguished men and women of both races in the United States. It has fought and won in state and federal courts, particularly in the United States Supreme Court, notable victories in defence of the citizenship rights of the Negro. Among these are victories against various forms of enforced residential segregation, restriction in the use of the ballot, attacks by mobs upon the homes of Negroes, and efforts to railroad Negroes to prison for defending themselves and their homes against such attacks, and in many cases where Negroes were through prejudice denied fair trials, as in the notable victory in the United States Supreme Court against peonage in Arkansas.

The outstanding accomplishment of the work of the N. A. A. C. P., as its rather long title is generally abbreviated, has been against lynching. It has investigated, through its officers and detectives, a great number of lynchings, for the Advancement Association realized that little confidence could be placed in the reports of such outbreaks in communities where officials and reporters were all too frequently in sympathy with the lynchers. The raw, unpleasant facts were unearthed by these investigators and in some instances the names of lynchers, in affidavits, were placed in the hands of law-enforcement officials. The failure of these officials to act in the great majority of cases has revealed as perhaps nothing else could the extent to which the habit of mobbism has fastened itself upon certain states, and the necessity of federal action.

The N. A. A. C. P. has made the facts about lynching familiar to the entire United States and to foreign countries through more than four thousand meetings; through the distribution of millions of pieces of literature, a number of them facsimile reproductions of stories of lynchings first printed in newspapers in the very communities in which they occurred; through *The Crisis*, edited by the distinguished Negro scholar, Dr. W. E. B. DuBois; and through an efficient press service, which goes weekly to each of the two hundred and fifty Negro newspapers and, when there is news of special interest to them, to white newspapers and news-distributing organizations throughout the world.

The N. A. A. C. P. also, in its campaign of education, compiled and published the only statistical study of lynching yet made, *Thirty Years of Lynching in the United States, 1889–1918,* and each year it keeps this record current through publication of a supplement. It has aided in the framing of a federal anti-lynching bill through its voluntary legal committee, composed of such eminent lawyers as Moorfield Storey, Louis Marshall, Arthur B. Spingarn, Clarence Darrow, James A. Cobb, Charles H. Studin, and Herbert K. Stockton. It has furnished members of Congress with the facts about lynching, and the use made of them in Congress has done an immense good in acquainting the public with the need of action. Notable among these facts have been those refuting the charge that all or most lynchings were in punishment of the crime of rape—the N. A. A. C. P. showing that less than one-fifth of the victims were even accused of that charge by the very mobs which lynched them.

The methods of the N. A. A. C. P. have not been gentle, for it was realized that a century-old public indifference to mob murders would not be penetrated by blandishments or by sugar-coating the facts. Naturally lynchers and their defenders have resented the unmasking of their deeds and have furiously assailed the N. A. A. C. P. with calumny and even vicious personal assault upon one of its white secretaries in Texas. None of these have deterred the movement for, in the words of its president, Moorfield Storey, the distinguished ex-president of the American Bar Association, and eminent authority on constitutional law, it realized that "it is not only working for colored people but to help the United States against the violence which is inevitable and is sure to cause disastrous consequences unless the supremacy of our principles and our laws can be restored." [1]

Through magazine articles, books, lectures, and personal contacts its officers, in addition to the means already detailed, have kept the issue of mobbism constantly before the public and thus helped to change apathy and hostility to interest and support of the campaign against Judge Lynch.

The second organization that has made great inroads upon the overwhelming ignorance and prejudice that surrounds the question of lynch-law is the Commission on Interracial Co-operation, with headquarters at Atlanta, home of the Ku Klux Klan and capital of the state with next to the greatest number of lynchings.

In *The Autobiography of an Ex-Coloured Man*, James Weldon Johnson gives this picture of the three classes into which Negroes in the United States are divided. The first and most generally known through newspaper mention is of loafers, ex-convicts, and the criminal type

---

[1] Quoted in a pamphlet, *The Rights of Minorities*, published by the N. A. A. C. P. (New York, 1928).

generally, who "hate everything covered with a white skin, and in return . . . are loathed by the whites"; the second class comprises servants "and all who are connected with the whites by domestic service"; and the third class is made up of "independent workmen and tradesmen, and of the well-to-do and educated coloured people," who "live in a little world of their own. In fact, I concluded that if a coloured man wanted to separate himself from his white neighbours, he had but to acquire some money, education, and culture. . . . The proudest and fairest lady in the South could with propriety—and it is what she would most likely do—go to the cabin of Aunt Mary, her cook, if Aunt Mary was sick, and minister to her comfort with her own hands; but if Mary's daughter, Eliza, a girl who used to run around my lady's kitchen, but who has received an education and married a prosperous young coloured man, were at death's door, my lady would no more think of crossing the threshold of Eliza's cottage than she would think of going into a bar-room for a drink."

The picture drawn thus in 1912 is, unfortunately, still largely true. Emphasis upon the shortcomings of a race and ignorance of those of the best of that race could not help creating a stereotype which has caused endless antagonism and misunderstanding. The Interracial Commission is designed to bridge such a chasm where such bridging is most needed—in the South. It seeks to bring together for conferences and action upon local interracial matters the most intelligent and representative members of each race.

This work has obviously not been easy of accomplishment in the face of the complex Southern situation, the fruit of three centuries of exploitation, injustice, and suspicion. There have been numerous instances where, gathered together "to talk frankly to each other," the white members have spoken freely of Negro faults and resented equal frankness by Negro members. There have been, too, those prominent in the movement—a notable example being Edwin Mims of Vanderbilt University in his *The Advancing South*—who take some pains in published writings to sneer at Negroes who are too outspoken for their taste in their analysis of the interracial situation. There has been as well a feeling that the Interracial Commission has not been so advanced in its program as even Southern conditions would warrant.

Such criticisms have become less justified as the movement has gained strength. It was organized shortly after the end of the World War, and by the end of 1926 had organized committees in upwards of eight hundred communities in fifteen states. One may gain an idea of the nature and method of work of the Commission against mob-law by these excerpts from its report for 1926:

> *Alabama*—Effective work for prevention of mob violence reported by Selma committee.

Georgia—Prevention of threatened lynching at Columbus through efforts of interracial group; number of irritating interracial situations adjusted. . . .

Kentucky—In two instances where lynching was feared, the State Commission called on governor and local officials for protection of prisoners; in both cases state militia was put on guard; and orderly trials conducted. In case of the one lynching in Kentucky the officer held responsible was removed by governor at request of Commission.

Tennessee—One hundred citizens of Dyersburg have signed pledges to assist sheriff at any time in protecting prisoners; have already functioned effectively in case of threatened violence. . . . [Dyersburg within recent years has been the scene of two of the most atrocious burnings on record.]

Texas—Prevention of two threatened lynchings reported from Walker County. . . .

Certain notorious states, such as Mississippi, Arkansas, Florida, and South Carolina, are noticeably absent from the list of those in which decent citizens are working against lynching, and the report quoted admits frankly lack of success in them. One might also object that the instances cited of lynchings prevented do not loom very large against the thirty-four lynchings which did occur in 1926. One may grant all this and yet see the value of the uphill but vital work which this movement is doing to change the thought-patterns of the South on this question.

Much more important than its work on immediate

cases of mob violence is that which the Commission is doing among Southern college students. Courses in race relations and the organization of voluntary study groups under the direction of members of the staff of the Commission, the furnishing of literature and the answering of questions, and the presentation of distinguished Negro speakers to audiences composed of Southern white college students are some of the methods by which this is done. Its pamphlets on *Negro Progress and Achievement, Popular Fallacies About Race Relations,* and *What the Bible Tells Me About Race Relations,* simply and informatively written, indicate the nature of the publications that are being used widely in this work.

The Commission is working with another group besides college students where there is hope of change of opinion—white women. One of its pamphlets, *Southern White Women on Lynching and Mob Violence,* details the vigorous repudiation by women of lynching as necessary for their protection. In Alabama white women have declared: "We protest . . . against the claim that lynching is necessary for the protection of white womanhood"; in Arkansas, "Recognizing with sympathetic appreciation the high standards of virtue set by the best element of colored women, we pledge ourselves to an effort to emphasize the single standard of morals for both men and women, that racial integrity may be assured, not to one race, but to both"; in Georgia, "We find in our hearts no extenuation for crime, be it in violation of womanhood, mob-violence, or the illegal taking of human life . . . we believe that 'no falser appeal can be made to Southern manhood than that mob-violence is necessary for the protection of womanhood' or that the brutal practice of lynching and burning of human beings is an expression of chivalry"; and like expressions have come from women in Kentucky, Louisiana, North Carolina, Oklahoma, South Carolina, Tennessee, Texas, and Virginia.

The dominant personality in the work of the Interracial Commission is Dr. Will W. Alexander, a former Methodist minister. Dr. Alexander has had associated with him some of the most liberal men of the South of both races—notably such men as the late John J. Eagan, the Rev. M. Ashby Jones, Dr. John Hope, Dr. Plato Durham, and Dr. Howard W. Odum.

There are other organizations that are indirectly attacking the problem of lynch-law which are helping to bring enlightenment. The Federal Council of Churches of Christ is conducting study groups, especially among women, on race relations. The Fellowship of Reconciliation, through the work of such a man as George L. Collins, is presenting to college students, North and South, sound, scientific information on race problems in general to replace the half-truths and myths on which many of these students have been fed in the past.

Significant, too, is the change that is to be seen among college and university students, white and coloured, through influences other than those already mentioned. It is, beyond all question, most evident at the University of North Carolina, owing to the work of such men as Howard Odum, Guy Johnson, Gerald W. Johnson (now on the staff of the Baltimore *Sun*), Paul Green, and Frederick Koch. Immensely valuable and important work in gathering, interpreting, and publishing little-known Negro secular and religious music has been done by Odum and Guy Johnson. Koch and Paul Green have through the medium of the drama helped to present, not only to the South, but to the entire country, certain aspects of Negro life. The approach of all these men has been remarkably free on the one hand from bias and condescension and on the other from sentimental eulogy of the Negro. Such an attitude has helped enormously to change many of the false ideas concerning the Negro which have in the past been so productive of evil results.

Each of these men has played a part, along with others less prominent in other Southern universities, towards the shaping of a movement that is bringing a new interpretation of Negro life to the American public. This movement is the utilization of Negro themes and Negro life by white and Negro artists in various fields. Roland Hayes, Paul Robeson, James Weldon Johnson, the late Florence Mills, Countee Cul-

len, Jean Toomer, Langston Hughes, Rudolph Fisher,
Rosamond Johnson, Taylor Gordon, Claude McKay,
Nella Larsen, Alain Locke, Eric Waldron, Aaron
Douglas, Julius Bledsoe, Marion Anderson, Rose Mc-
Clendon, Charles Gilpin, W. E. B. DuBois, Frank
Wilson, and a number of other Negro singers, writers,
painters, poets, and actors have achieved phenomenal
success within recent years. That success has done much
towards giving an entirely new picture of Negro life—
one which already has helped to create an understanding
and respect which could not have been created in a similar period in any other fashion. To the work of these
have been added novels and short stories by T. S. Strib-
ling, Julia Peterkin, Dubose Heyward, and Carl Van
Vechten; plays by Eugene O'Neill, Paul Green, Ridgley
Torrence; informative, sympathetic, and scholarly volumes on Negro music and folklore by Howard Odum
and Guy Johnson. Many of these writers are of the
South, and, though their work is naturally of varying
merit, each of them is leagues ahead of workers in other
fields who have the Negro as subject.

In *The Mauve Decade* Thomas Beer tells of a hot-
headed young Georgian, son of a minister, who was a
teacher at Vanderbilt University. One day he was hor-
rified to find that certain of his fellow faculty-members
not only believed in, but were actually teaching, biology
according to Haeckel. At the height of an indignant
protest to Lindon Cabell Garland, the chancellor of the

university, against such heresy, he was interrupted by the older man with the quiet remark: "Men never amount to much until they outgrow their fathers' notions, sir." These writers, white and coloured, are helping towards the abandonment of their father's notions of race, science, religion, politics, and a great many other subjects. If this seed of ferment and honest scepticism can be kept alive in the South, there is some hope for a new day below the Mason and Dixon line.

Back of the changes already noted lie two factors which, more than any other, have tended towards revolutionizing Southern thought upon lynching and the Negro. These are the migration from the South of nearly a million and a half Negroes between 1916 and 1928; and the increasing resistance by Negroes to mob attacks.

When the World War began, in 1914, the United States was receiving from European countries each year upwards of a million immigrants. The war came, and, in the words of Charles S. Johnson, the brilliant young editor of *Opportunity: A Journal of Negro Life*, now at Fisk University, "the cities of the North, stern, impersonal and enchanting, needed men of the brawny muscles, which Europe, suddenly flaming with war, had ceased to supply, when the black hordes came on from the South like a silent, encroaching shadow." The movement of this vast army of black workers to Chicago, Pittsburgh, Detroit, Cleveland, and other industrial cen-

tres to replace Poles and Lithuanians, Croatians and
Austrians and other European races was at first greeted
with joy in the South—"now that we're getting rid of
the niggers we'll have nothing but peace," some said.
Then came a not so comfortable, joyous feeling when it
was found that a maid or a cook could not be hired with
the old ease and at the old wages. This gave way to con-
sternation when vast areas, especially after a lynching,
were depopulated overnight. The South was learning
for the first time the value of the asset it had in Negro
labour.

The situation was met in two ways. The old South
fell back on its old stand-by—violence. Labour agents
were flogged, run out of town, confronted with a fan-
tastically high licence-fee. Negroes were beaten and
lynched, railroad tickets destroyed. These methods
served not inconsiderably in speeding the parting Negroes and helping to make up the minds of those who
were yet debating whether to leave. The more intelligent South, on the other hand, began to show signs of
awakening to the gravity of the situation. They realized
that, now that the Negroes had a place to which they
could go for freedom from lynching and insult, for decent wages, living conditions, and school facilities, they
would require more decent treatment in the South or
they would leave. This realization led to the strengthen-
ing of the work of the Interracial Commission, to plans

for better schools for Negroes in states like North Carolina and Louisiana, to much more outspoken condemnation of lynching by the press and the better element of the public. Whatever the conditions found and
created in the North by the migrants, no considerable
percentage of those who had left the South were returning. Thus the movement towards betterment of
Southern conditions gained a permanency instead of
expiring when the high point of the migratory movement had passed.

The effect upon the Negro, North and South, of this
new opportunity was very significant. There came a stif-
fening of resistance to oppression with the hope of
better conditions. Not only in Chicago and Washington,
where Negroes met the mob resolved to die fighting, but
in isolated sections of the South the same attitude was
to be seen. In some instances the new type of Negro
meant an increase in the size of the mob; in some a
greater savagery in the excution of the victim. In others
it meant that mobs were a shade more hesitant about
taking summary vengeance—it was not so comfortable
to reflect that someone might get hurt or even killed,
and the individual in the mob did not relish the thought
that this someone might be himself. In the North, for
example, there had been a large number of bombings
and other attacks upon homes of Negroes until the fall
of 1925, when a member of the mob that was attacking

the home of a Negro physician in Detroit was killed. The attacks ceased, not only in Detroit, but throughout the country.

Another factor is the changing condition being wrought in the South by business, the radio, the automobile, and good roads, which are breaking up the old South and creating new thought-patterns. Dr. Alexander of the Interracial Commission tersely sums up this new situation in these words: "Today the South reads Associated Press dispatches, national advertising, and listens each night to national radio programs. The heroes of southern boys today are General Pershing, Ford, Edison and Lindbergh. The Prince Albert coat and the goatee have entirely disappeared. The Rotarian, true to the national type, is the voice of the community. What the nation thinks the South is largely thinking; that America is God's country and Calvin Coolidge is a great president."

This new situation, born of changing industrial and economic conditions, and bringing with it whatever it may, is slowly changing, according to Dr. Alexander, the political philosophy of the South, breaking up the old isolation, and giving the South something else to think about in place of its traditional emotional fixation on the Negro. Having realized through the migration the economic asset that the Negro is to the South, and the disastrous economic effect of mob-law and the re-

sulting disturbance of white and Negro labour, this new
and powerful force of enlightened self-interest is working and will work for suppression of mobbism—that
is, where mobbism works against pecuniary interest.

Ironically, the organization designed primarily to
suppress Negro accomplishment, the Ku Klux Klan, has
unwittingly helped to lower the lynching rate. This does
not refer to the Klan's boast that it has checked lynchings, for there is no record of anything except to the
contrary. It does refer to the agitation of the Klan for
an "America for Americans" and laws for restriction
of immigration. Their efforts in this direction, coupled
with those of the American Federation of Labor and
of the considerable element of Americans who are sus-
picious of foreign entanglements, have helped to solid-
ify the Negro's place in American labour, by lessening
the considerable competition of unrestricted immigration.

Somewhat further back in the anti-lynching movement come the churches. The distressingly high percentage of ignorant, prejudiced ministers in the white
Southern church offers the most discouraging aspect of
the entire problem of lynching and race relations, as
well as in the task of enlightenment in general. The
hold that such ministers have upon the great masses of
Southern whites, especially in the rural regions, as has

already been seen, explains in large measure such re-trogressive movements as the Klan, Fundamentalism, anti-science and anti-Northern agitation. These preach-ers are shrewd enough to know that if their followers were reasonably enlightened, they themselves would be without jobs. They thus play on every fear, every pas-sion, every stupidity of those they profess to lead. It is in such an atmosphere as these men create that a Texas preacher killed a man in cold blood on a Saturday afternoon and then faced his congregation the following morning, taking as his text: "There is therefore now no condemnation to them which are in Christ Jesus."

Some of the leaders of the Interracial Commission are ministers and there are a few courageous ministers and bishops who have taken an active stand against lynching. Unfortunately they are all too rare. A prom-inent Southerner who was formerly connected with the church analyses the situation in these words: "The church, officially, nearly always follows economic and political trends rather than oppose them . . . over-emphasis on creeds and opinion" and "insistence on the importance of theological opinion," combined with prejudice, effectively checking courageous action against lynching precisely as the same forces checked church action against slavery. A pulpit and the mantle of au-thority that still robes the minister give exaggerated importance to prejudice and intolerance which these men hold in common with many of their congregations.

Little may be hoped for from the present generation of ministers, it would appear, in the fight to end the
rule of the mob. There does seem, however, to be
ground for optimism in the attitude of the newer group
of young ministers who are today learning in the seminaries something of the Negro and who are subject to
the enlightening influences that are touching the South.

These, then, seem to be some of the more significant
evidences of changes that are taking place today towards at least an abatement of the evil of lynching. One
might object that all of them together represent but a
fraction of American public opinion. That is true, yet
they are of immense importance when one considers
that two decades ago there was practically no opposition, organized or unorganized, against mob-law. Lecky,
the English historian, once wrote of the American
Revolution that it "was the work of an energetic minority
who succeeded in committing an undecided and fluctuat-
ing majority to courses for which they had little love
and leading them step by step to a position from which
it was impossible to recede." It is not, perhaps, a wholly
malapropos analogy to the lynching situation. For the
question now seems to be whether the energetic minority
at work against lynch-law can overcome the serious
handicap of a century of practically unchecked mob
violence and end what is, without exaggeration, the most
serious problem in American life.

CHAPTER NINE

LYNCHINGS AND LAWS: IS THERE A WAY OUT?

═══════

IT IS a truism that no public evil is ever ended until there is marshalled a potent if not considerable public opinion behind a movement to put an end to the evil. Contrariwise, agitation for legal weapons against the condition complained of constitutes the most effective means of creating such organized opposition to the evil. The history of lynching offers an excellent example of the truth of these statements, and especially of the value of agitation for state and federal laws against the practice.

Such progress as has been made has come in the face of almost insuperable obstacles, not least of which was general indifference. Lynching, like its parent, slavery, has become more or less firmly fixed in American psychology. Among other naïve delusions of the average American is one of himself as a virile, rough-and-ready superman of the rugged, pioneer type, infinitely superior to the effete citizens of other countries. While this type is more noticeable in the rural South, his counterpart exists in every section of the United States. He will be found in the grandstand or bleachers of any baseball

park, safely among his fellows, yelling: "Kill the um-
pire!" When a truck-driver runs over a child playing
in the streets of even so cosmopolitan a city as New
York, the tendency of the American is to explode instantly into cries of "Lynch him!" and "String him up!"
In times of unusual excitement, as when a war is being
waged, he is trigger-quick to shout: "Pro-German!" or
"Bolshevik!" and to recommend instant lynching; or,
among the more timid: "They ought to be sent back
to where they came from!" When lurid stories of real
or alleged crime-waves arouse hysteria, as in the
Leopold-Loeb or Sacco-Vanzetti cases, a considerable
percentage of citizens of the United States can think
of no other solution to the problems involved than "They
ought to be taken out and strung up to the nearest
telegraph-pole!" or "They ought to be tarred and feathered!" The chief difference between the states where
there are many lynchings and those where there are few
would seem to be police efficiency, and the freedom from
mob violence which comes from that effectiveness.

Earle Fiske Young, of the University of Southern
California, presents evidence of the truth of this assertion in *Sociology and Social Research* for March–April,
1928 (Vol. XII, No. 4). He tabulates lynchings over a
period of thirty years in fourteen Southern states by
population rates of counties in these states, and thus
works out a relation of lynching to the size of political
areas. The states studied are Alabama, Arkansas,

Florida, Georgia, Kentucky, Louisiana, Mississippi, Missouri, North Carolina, Oklahoma, South Carolina, Tennessee, Texas, and Virginia. Professor Young found that the rate of lynchings (not the *number* of persons lynched, which would have made the figures even more striking) was inversely as the populousness of the counties.

Counties of less than 10,000 inhabitants were found to have a lynching rate of 3.2; of 10,000 to 20,000 a rate of 2.4; of 20,000 to 30,000 a rate of 2.1; of 30,-000 to 40,000 a rate of 1.7; of 40,000 to 50,000 a rate of 2.4; of 50,000 to 100,000 a rate of 1.0; of 100,-000 to 200,000 a rate of 0.6; of 200,000 to 300,000 a rate of 0.3; and of 300,000 to 800,000 a rate of only 0.05.

Such figures, Professor Young believes, show that increasing the size of political areas, as was contemplated by various proposed federal laws against lynching, would result in more efficient administration of governmental functions and in overcoming local feelings and prejudices. Whether such a result would really follow or not remains to be seen. But Professor Young's figures do tend to prove that the bigotry, intolerance, and racial animosities of the rural South offer the most difficult of all problems in seeking to end lynching and mob violence.

Against so general a tendency to take the law into the hands of the mob, "educating public opinion" is an uphill climb. To attain any appreciable success in the effort to end all lynching within a reasonably short period requires the expenditure of an enormous amount of energy, devotion, intelligence, and money. As has already been pointed out, point and direction to such efforts have been given by the goal of state or federal legislation against lynchers. Since the early nineties there have been resolutions, bills, and laws in various state legislatures and in Congress. The fitful discussion aroused by these measures has helped to stir a sluggish public opinion and, being cumulative in its effect, has done much towards impressing upon the public the necessity of ending so terrible an evil. For most of the laws passed this is the utmost that may be said in their favour. The majority of them have been poorly framed, ineffective, superficial, and incapable of enforcement. This has been especially true in those states where rabid colour prejudice prevented the forming of sufficient sentiment for enforcement.

State Laws

On March 14, 1891 eleven Italians were lynched at New Orleans for alleged conspiracy to murder. These lynchings led to an exceedingly tense situation between Italy and the United States, diplomatic intercourse actually being severed during the controversy. The breach was eventually closed through payment by the United States of damages to the amount of $24,330.90. So

severe was the criticism heaped upon Louisiana because
of this that the Louisiana state legislature was petitioned
in strong language by prominent citizens of the state to
pass a law against lynching. Nothing was done by the
legislature, but the petition was significant as one of
the first instances where lynching was recognized as a
crime that required special legislation.

So serious a menace to the public welfare had lynching become that other states were also casting about for
some possible relief. In 1891 mobs had killed 195 persons, in 1892 the number of victims rose sharply to
235, in 1893 there were 200 victims, and 197 in 1894.
These wholesale murders led to petitions to a number
of legislatures, and a number of governors in their
messages to these bodies included requests for special
legislation to curb lynchers. Governor Atkinson of
Georgia made a recommendation which had more merit
than any of the· others, and which would have acted as
a powerful deterrent to mobs. His suggestion was that
sheriffs or other peace officers in charge of a prisoner
whom a mob demanded be required, should the officer
be unable or unwilling to protect his prisoner, to remove the handcuffs, arm the prisoner, and permit him
to defend his own life. Mobs being made up of cowards, the Governor's reasoning ran, they went forth
to mutilate and slay only because they felt certain that
no one but the victim would be hurt or killed. Though
the odds against an armed prisoner be ten thousand

to one, the possibility that *one* of the mobbists might be killed would cause each member of the mob to reflect: "That one person might be *me!*" Governor Atkinson's suggestion was not acted upon.

In 1893 the Georgia legislature did pass an act of doubtful value and cryptic phrasing. It provided for imprisonment of from one to twenty years of any person found guilty of "mobbing or lynching any citizen . . . without due process of law," and authorized a sheriff to require service of any citizen to help protect a prisoner threatened with lynching. Whether through intention or ineptness, the wording of the bill implied that there might be a mobbing or lynching *with* due process of law. The law, so far as can be ascertained, had little if any effect in checking lynchings.

The North Carolina legislature in the same year enacted a law that sought to evade the difficulties of trying an alleged lyncher in his own county, where his friends or relatives or sympathizers might be on the jury. This measure gave jurisdiction to the superior court of any county adjoining that in which the lynching occurred, and, among other provisions, provided a fine or imprisonment or both for any person who broke into a jail for the purpose of lynching a prisoner. Though better framed, this law was no more effective than that of Georgia. Adjoining counties were too close to obtain impartial jurors—many of the residents were participants in or sympathizers with the lynching. The penalty for breaking into a jail to obtain a prisoner was of little effect other than to cause mobs to seize their victims before they could be incarcerated. The most intelligent part of the bill was that which was aimed at a very vulnerable point—the taxpayers and the county treasury. This provided that the entire cost of the proceedings should be borne by the county in which the lynching occurred, and if an insufficient guard had been placed about the victim, the county was liable for damages to the next of kin of the deceased. This clause was one of the first instances where punitive damages were provided, and the principle has since been held constitutional by various state supreme courts and has acted as a potent deterrent to lynch-law. Weakness of other parts of the North Carolina statute, however, nullified this part of the act.

In 1895 Georgia sought to strengthen the act passed in 1893 by providing penalties for persons who obstructed a sheriff or his deputy in protecting a prisoner from a mob. There is no record that the added provision helped to meet the issue.

South Carolina during the same year adopted a new state constitution, in which provision was made for the removal of a sheriff by the governor when that officer was negligent in protecting a prisoner against lynching; and for damages of two thousand dollars to the next of kin of the victim from the county in which the lynching took place. The latter provision has been fulfilled in several cases of lynching in South Carolina and has tended materially towards checking lynching. The former provision, however, has been practically worthless. This was seen most clearly in the notorious and bestial triple lynching at Aiken in 1926. The governor can suspend a sheriff only upon indictment of that officer, and remove him only upon conviction. The sheriff at Aiken was named in numerous affidavits, not only as doing nothing to protect the three prisoners, *but as an actual participant in the lynchings.* The grand jury refused to indict, despite the evidence, and the sheriff retained his job.

Ohio in 1896 followed by passing an act that provided, in addition to the usual penalties, for damages to any person beaten or manhandled by a mob after being taken from an officer, of one thousand dollars from the county in which the assault took place; for damages of five hundred dollars to any person attacked by a mob and slightly injured; of one thousand dollars if more seriously injured; and of five thousand dollars if permanently disabled; and in the case of a lynching, damages of five thousand dollars to the next of kin. The Ohio statute also provided damages to any person injured by a mob in search of another, and, in the event of an innocent person's being killed in such circumstances, damages to his legal representative in the same amount as though the deceased had been the object of the mob's search. This act was amended two years later by the addition of special penalties for persons who attacked or entered a jail for the purpose of taking a person to be lynched.

In 1897 three states—Kentucky, Texas, and Tennessee—and in 1899 Indiana passed anti-lynching laws of various degrees of merit, largely based on the enactments already mentioned. Michigan in 1899 added a law against lynching which was modelled on the Ohio statute, but repealed it four years afterwards. Alabama in 1901 provided through her constitution for impeachment of a sheriff or his deputy who permitted a prisoner to be taken from him and lynched; and upon conviction he was made ineligible "to hold any office in this State during the time for which he had been elected to serve as sheriff." Kansas in 1903 authorized payment of rewards for apprehension and punishment of lynchers and enacted an anti-lynching measure. During recent years Kentucky, Florida, and West Virginia have given their governors authority to remove negligent sheriffs. In Kentucky's one lynching in 1926 the negligent officer was removed by the Governor under the provisions of that state's anti-lynching law.

The effect of these laws need not be judged by the number of times they have been used successfully to punish lynchers. The best laws are those that prevent crime instead of punishing it. Even the most optimistic person, however, would be compelled to admit that the history of state laws against lynching is, at best, a record of questionable effectiveness. The states with the worst lynching records either will not pass laws against the evil or, in those few which have such laws, find it practically impossible to enforce them, especially when the victim is a Negro. The acid test of all the assertions that the states can and will enact and enforce anti-lynching laws is this: Can the lynchers of Negroes be indicted, tried, and if found guilty, punished? The answer to date is in the negative. The Supreme Courts of Ohio, Alabama, Kansas, and South Carolina have upheld the validity of damages against counties in which lynchings have taken place, but grand juries and the lower courts, especially of states where most of the lynchings have occurred, refuse to act against lynchers even when the evidence is clear.

In brief, we are yet a long way from prompt and unbiased action against lynchers by grand juries and the courts of a considerable number of states. The extent and the viciousness of race prejudice in the lynching states make it exceedingly doubtful whether or not it will be possible for many years to come to obtain convictions of lynchers in state courts of those states when the victim is a Negro. Agitation for the passage of state laws is valuable in its educational effect, but there are certain reasons for doubting the efficacy of state laws in ending lynching within a reasonable period. The chief weaknesses of such laws would appear to be (1) that where they are most needed, the very sentiment which causes lynching makes enactment and enforcement of such laws impossible; (2) that juries drawn from the county in which the lynching occurred or counties near by are more than likely to have upon them relatives, friends, fellow participants, or sympathizers of the defendants who would refuse to vote for convictions; and (3) that provisions for removal of negligent sheriffs or deputies by the governor, while valuable, are nullified when grand juries or lower courts refuse to indict or convict such officers; and, obviously, there is danger in giving a governor power of removal based solely upon his own judgment as to whether or not the sheriff did sincerely attempt to protect his prisoner. In brief, state anti-lynching laws are valuable and effective in an inverse ratio to the need for them.

There is no desire to disparage sincere efforts for enactment and enforcement of state laws against the evil of lynching. For reasons already given, they have both a direct and an indirect value. Unsentimental examination of the question causes one to conclude, however, that for such states as Mississippi, Arkansas, Florida, and others of the lower South there is little hope of effective action against lynchers through this channel. Until the lyncher of any person, regardless of the colour of the victim's skin or the offence with which he is charged, can be promptly indicted, tried, and convicted, state laws in such states are an illusion—and no honest citizen can assert that they will not continue to be in this generation and in several to come. And, while the day when such laws will be effective is perhaps coming, there are living in those states human beings, perhaps yet unborn, who are to be the victims of the rope and the faggot.

Proposals for Federal Action

Attempts to curb lynchings by means of federal action began about the same time as proposals for state laws against the practice. The late Senator George F. Hoar of Massachusetts, who fought valiantly against American imperialism in the Philippines, was the author of one of the first bills to give the federal Government jurisdiction against lynchers. In 1902 there was introduced in the House of Representatives a bill designed to throw federal protection against lynching around aliens resident in the United States. Up to that time in various parts of the United States mobs had lynched Italians, Chinese, Japanese, Bohemians, Mexicans, and citizens of Great Britain and Switzerland. As a result the United States Government had paid in the fifteen years between 1887 and 1901 a total of $475,-499.90 in indemnities to the Governments of China, Italy, Great Britain, and Mexico; in 1903 an additional sum of $5000 was paid to Italy for the lynching in Mississippi of a citizen of that country. The bill introduced in Congress in 1902, upon which no action was taken, was designed to protect aliens and did not attempt to touch upon the question of the lynching of citizens of the United States.

Within recent years there has come a revival of such measures, along with the growing agitation against mob-law. Emphasis has properly been shifted in all of these measures to protect American citizens as well as those of foreign countries. Among them the bill introduced by Congressman L. C. Dyer of Missouri and backed by the National Association for the Advancement of Colored People and other organizations has received most thoughtful attention.

Before proceeding to a brief analysis of the provisions of the Dyer Bill and others like it, it may perhaps be interesting to point out some of the anomalous situations that perplex those who are seeking honestly to find some way by which the Government of the United States may protect its own citizens from lynching in those states where the local courts and officials are helpless against the mob. For example, no less an authority than the Chief Justice of the United States Supreme Court, William Howard Taft, is responsible for the statement that a federal law to punish the lynchers of aliens is constitutional and that in the failure to enact such legislation "we may well hang our heads in the face of adverse criticism"; [1] but Chief Justice Taft

[1] *Aliens and Their Treaty Rights.* Printed in *Hearings Before the Committee on the Judiciary, House of Representatives, Sixty-sixth Congress, Second Session, on H. R. 259, 4123, and 11873.* Government Printing Office, Washington, 1920, p. 15.

and other eminent authorities on constitutional law feel that "for lynchings of our own citizens within the jurisdiction of the State we can say to ourselves for we have no other plea, that under the form of our government such crimes are a State matter, and if the people of a State will not provide, for their own protection, a machinery in the administration of justice that will prevent such lawless violence, and a public opinion to make it effective, then it is for them to bear the ignominy of such a condition."

To the man who is interested in humanity instead of fine shadings of legal reasoning, in equal justice instead of law, such distinctions and such confessions of federal helplessness bear an ironic tinge. This is especially true when he considers that the principal victims of lynching are disfranchised by chicanery and impudent use of lynch-law itself, and are thus unable to "provide, for their protection, a machinery . . . that will prevent such lawless violence, and a public opinion to make it effective." Once again will such a man be impressed with the lack of synonymity between law as such and common humaneness.

Another anomalous situation perplexes the lay mind. The United States Supreme Court has ruled (*Logan* v. *United States*, 144 *U. S.* 263) that one who kills a prisoner who is in the custody of a federal officer may be punished for murder by the United States. Let us state a hypothetical case based on this decision. A citizen of the United States, for example, is charged with counterfeiting or the murder of a federal judge on his way to hold court in another place, or with committing some crime in a post office. He is arrested by a United States marshal, who starts with his prisoner to jail. A mob, *off* of government property, takes the prisoner and lynches him. The full power of the United States can be used to arrest and punish each of the lynchers for murder. But let us suppose that the prisoner took exactly one step off of government property and committed a crime not against federal law. He is arrested, not by a federal officer (for whatever consolation that may be to his kinsmen), but by a sheriff or policeman. A mob takes him and burns him at the stake. Under our present laws and constitution his citizenship even in his own country is worthless so far as federal power is concerned, either in protecting him from lynching or in punishing his lynchers.

Such elementary examples of legalistic hair-splitting are most vexing to those who are concerned with putting an end to lynching and not with debating exceedingly fine points of law. This vexation is all the more annoying when, as distinguished from those who have honest doubts as to the power of the federal Government to act in the matter of mob-law, there are those who blatantly defend lynching and, in doing so, utilize legal technicalities to prevent action against lynchers. A notorious example of such tactics was seen in the

United States Senate in 1922 when, after the House of Representatives had passed by a vote of 230 to 119 the Dyer Anti-Lynching Bill, such Southern senators as John Sharp Williams and Pat Harrison of Mississippi, the late Oscar Underwood of Alabama, Thaddeus Caraway of Arkansas, and other senators from states where lynchings have been most numerous prevented by a filibuster even discussion of lynching. It is only fair to add that considerable aid was given to them by certain Northern and Republican senators (such as the late Henry Cabot Lodge) who were renegade to promises to their constituents to combat the filibuster. The net result of such efforts is to obscure public opinion upon an issue already obscured to the point of opaqueness. The progress that certain states boast of will never be evident until the electors of those states choose a higher type of individual to represent them, to replace those who add to a difficult situation cheap appeals to the basest of racial prejudices and passions.

Dismissing those of this class, there remain for consideration the arguments of those who honestly doubt the constitutionality of a federal anti-lynching law, however well framed, and of those who are convinced that such a law can be framed so as to be both effective and constitutional. First, there are those who contend that lynching is murder and nothing more and that punishment lies wholly and solely upon state governments for murder, whether it be committed by one or by ten thousand persons. In answer to those who hold such an opinion, James Weldon Johnson testified at a hearing of the Judiciary Committee of the United States Senate in 1926 in these words: "The chief constitutional objection to such legislation is that the federal Government has no more warrant to step in to punish lynching in the States than it has to prevent or punish any other form of murder or any other crime—arson, for example. I think it is safe to say that lynching is not simply murder; that it is murder plus something else. It is murder plus revolution and anarchy. It is murder plus a flaunting and overthrowing and trampling under foot of the prerogatives of the courts. The mob apprehends the victim, tries and condemns, and then executes him. That is, in committing murder the mob arrogates to itself the rights and powers of the courts."

There is also the contention that even should lynching be regarded as a special form of murder, there is not the authority in the Constitution to give the federal government through its courts jurisdiction over the crime. This argument is met by Herbert K. Stockton of New York in a brief, the most comprehensive upon the question of such legislation, which was filed in 1926 and reprinted in the report of hearings before the Senate Judiciary Committee. Since Mr. Stockton's brief, filed on behalf of the National Association for the Advancement of Colored People, is so comprehensive, it affords the best and fullest exposition of the moot legal questions on which centres most of the discussion of federal anti-lynching legislation. An effort, therefore, will be made to summarize here the main contentions.

It is set forth at the outset that Congress has the power to enact such legislation through the fourteenth amendment to the Constitution and specifically through the provision which reads: "Nor shall any State . . . deny to any person within its jurisdiction the equal protection of the laws"; and under that amendment's supplementary section 5, which empowers Congress to enforce the provision quoted by appropriate legislation. Such legislation would not supersede or nullify state action against lynchers, since federal action would, under the bill's provisions, be possible only in certain contingencies; "when the State or county officers do not try to prevent or punish a lynching they are criminally liable, the county is made subject to a fine [of $10,000] and the Federal court, with its jury drawn from a broader district than the county panel, shall try the lynchers." Instead of relieving the States from the task of preventing and punishing lynchings, they are given every inducement and opportunity to act *before* the federal power would be operative.

United States Supreme Court decisions are then cited to establish that the federal Government has not only the right, but the obligation as well, to assure to all its citizens their rights as citizens, which include equal protection of the laws, and to prevent encroachment by the states or by individuals upon those rights. Lynching figures are cited to support the contention that the mobs' victims do not get equal protection of the laws of the states, that state and county officials do not try to prevent this crime as they do others, and that they do not try to punish his crime as they do other crimes. It is contended that these constitute inequality of protection, gross neglect on the part of state authorities whose duty it is to afford equal protection, and, in the failure of those officers, a failure of the state itself.

That such failure is in violation of the fourteenth amendment and that the federal Government is obligated to afford such protection when the individual states fail to do so is asserted upon the basis of certain notable decisions of the Federal Supreme Court. Among these is that in the case of Saunders *v.* Shaw (244 *U. S.* 317, 320), where the court said that "the denial of rights given by the fourteenth amendment need not be by legislation"; and, in another case, that "such an actual discrimination is as potential in creating a denial of equality of rights as a discrimination made by law"—this latter case referring to the barring of Negroes from jury duty (*Tarrance* v. *Florida*, 188 *U. S.* 519). The Supreme Court has also ruled, it is pointed out, that the federal Government has the right to inquire whether a state law, fair enough on its surface, has back of it prejudice that will cause denial of equal protection in its administration (*Yick Wo* v. *Hopkins*,

118 *U. S.* 356). These and other decisions are cited to establish the facts that (1) equal protection of the laws as contemplated by the fourteenth amendment is not being given, particularly to Negroes, who are the principal victims of lynching; and that (2) the state is responsible for the action or non-action of each and all of its officials charged with the enforcement of the law down to "the most obscure subordinate in the State's governmental organization."

Whether or not the anti-lynching bill then being discussed was "appropriate legislation" in enforcing the Constitutional prohibition of denial of equal protection was next considered. The validity of federal action against individuals within a state whose duty it is to give equal protection of the laws, but who have failed to do so, action against them being equivalent to action against the state itself, is affirmed upon the basis of such decisions as that in Strauder *v.* West Virginia (100 *U. S.* 303, 306, 310), where the Supreme Court specifically declared: "A State acts by its legislative, its executive, or its judicial authorities. It can act in no other way. The constitutional provision, therefore, must mean that no agency of the State, or of the officers or agents by whom its powers are exerted, shall deny to any person within its jurisdiction the equal protection of the laws." [2]

[2] Other decisions of the United States Supreme Court to the same effect quoted by Mr. Stockton are: Virginia *v.* Rives, 100 *U. S.* 318;

That it is appropriate legislation to enforce constitutional provisions forbidding the states to deny equal
protection of its laws is shown by such decisions as those
in Logan *v.* United States, and Virginia *v.* Rives. In the
latter the Supreme Court declared that "Congress, by
virtue of the fifth section of the fourteenth amendment,
may enforce the prohibitions whenever they are disre-
garded by either the legislative, the executive, or the
judicial department of the State. The mode of enforcement is left to its discretion." And in the Cruikshank case
(1 *Woods Circuit Court Reports,* 315) Mr. Justice
Bradley declared: "It seems to be firmly established
by the unanimous opinion of the judges . . . that
Congress has power to enforce by appropriate legislation every right and privilege given by or guaranteed
by the Constitution."

The brief contends that such decisions warrant belief
in the right of Congress to pass anti-lynching legislation,
in the face of the open and notorious denial of equal
protection of the laws as evidenced by close to five
thousand lynchings over a period of less than half a
century.

The clause of the anti-lynching bill providing for punishment of lynchers who conspire with officials to lynch
is justified under the legal principles applicable to con-
spiracies, such persons being regarded as principals,

Ex Parte Virginia, 100 *U. S.* 339; Raymond *v.* Chicago Traction Co.,
207 *U. S.* 35, 36; Home Telegraph & Telephone Co. *v.* Los Angeles, 227
U. S., p. 278.

as in Cohen *v.* United States (157 *Fed.* 651); authority for giving federal courts jurisdiction in prosecuting individual members of mobs when state officials fail to do their duty is affirmed by decisions already quoted and especially in such cases as Virginia *v.* Rives. Provisions for fines upon counties in which lynchings take place are shown to have ample precedents in various state statutes and decisions of state supreme courts affirming the validity of such fines, as we have already seen in South Carolina, Ohio, Alabama, and Kansas. The validity of the inclusion of a clause applying to aliens, as well as citizens of the United States, who might be lynched is next briefly dealt with under the treaty power of the federal Government.

The brief concludes with a comparison of the decisions of the United States Supreme Court in the famous Leo Frank case (*Frank* v. *Mangum,* 237 *U. S.* 309, 335) and those arising from the Elaine, Arkansas, riots of October 1919 (*Moore* v. *Dempsey,* 261 *U. S.* 86). In the latter case the Supreme Court reversed an Arkansas court which had dismissed a writ of habeas corpus granted to Negroes who had been convicted in a trial completely dominated by a mob, making any other verdict than conviction impossible despite the evidence. The Supreme Court said, in effect, that even though a state went through all the *form* of a trial, if it could be shown that mob spirit against the defendants was so strong as to prejudice that court, the federal

Government had authority to go behind the trial itself and declare it null and void—practically a complete reversal of the Supreme Court's decision in the Leo Frank case.

"The implications of this decision," the brief concludes, "are of significance in connection with such legislation as is proposed herewith, because in such a case the United States Supreme Court examines into the State court trial, and, regardless of the approval of that trial by the State court of appeal, determines for itself whether or not the proceedings were dominated by the mob, so as not to constitute due process of law. Upon so finding, the Federal court will take action directly with regard to the individuals involved so as to make good to them the constitutional guaranty under the fourteenth amendment that the State shall not deprive them of life or liberty without due process of law.

"In analogous fashion the present bill will, we confidently believe, be upheld as appropriate legislation to make good the guaranty of the fourteenth amendment to those who suffer from the unequal administration of the State laws, which now fail to protect them from the lynching mobs. Such an appeal to this legislative body, which represents all the people of this country and which is commanded by the highest law of the land to see that none of them is denied the equal protection of the laws of the States, must not fall on deaf ears."

So short a summary of this brief necessarily means
the elimination of much that would be valuable to quote.
Enough has been given, however, to indicate the grounds
upon which proponents of federal anti-lynching legislation base their belief as to the constitutionality of the
measure now pending before Congress. Certainly there
is enough foundation and more for Mr. Stockton's modest "reasonable certainty" that should the bill become
law and a test case be carried to that tribunal, the United
States Supreme Court will rule in its favour. As has been
said, there are other honest and eminent lawyers who do
not agree wholly with the reasoning of the brief quoted.
Among them is Moorfield Storey of Boston, a former
president of the American Bar Association, president
since its formation of the National Association for the
Advancement of Colored People, and one of the greatest
authorities on constitutional law in the United States.
In 1920 Mr. Storey wrote to Congressman Frederick W.
Dallinger of Massachusetts, author of an anti-lynching
bill which was later consolidated with that of Congressman Dyer, in these words:

"It has seemed to me a very doubtful question
whether legislation by Congress against lynching in the
States is constitutional, but I am very clearly of the
opinion that it ought to be tried. I think the South ex-
pects it, and many of our Southern citizens who are
opposed to lynching will welcome it. . . . A murder,
in the ordinary course of things, is an offense wholly

within the jurisdiction of the State, and if the authorities of the State do their best to prevent such offenses or to punish the offenders the United States cannot, in my judgment, interfere. If, however, the authorities do not prosecute the offenders in earnest, or if, like the governor of Mississippi the other day, when advised that a lynching was to take place, they profess absolute inability to act, then it would seem to me that the Government should step in. I hope your act will be reported favorably by the committee and that it may become a law, for I feel very sure that unless lynching of colored people is stopped we are drifting into what may well become civil war."

There would, perhaps, be a closer approach between the two groups who honestly disagree on the question of effective steps towards abolition of lynching were there not the third class, already mentioned, composed of those who wave the bloody shirt and appeal to racial and sectional prejudices in defending lynching while masking their real purpose by use of arguments regarding constitutionality and "states' rights." It would seem reasonable, however, should lynching continue, that the experiment of federal legislation be tried and the moot point of constitutionality be referred through a test case to the only authority that can finally decide it—the Supreme Court of the United States.

Such action has been recommended in various fashions by presidents of the United States from Benjamin

Harrison in 1891, following the lynching of the Italians at New Orleans, through the list to Wilson, Harding, and Coolidge. There are various possible benefits, direct and indirect, from enactment of an adequate federal law of this nature.

Nothing would serve so effectively to lessen the present self-esteem of lynchers. It would serve notice upon them that a roused public opinion no longer approved of their deeds and was determined to put an end to their immunity.

Such a law would demonstrate to the world at large that the United States is not as indifferent to or as helpless in the face of the activities of lynching mobs as now, with justice, is thought. Arthur B. Spingarn of New York, testifying in 1920 before the Judiciary Committee of the House of Representatives of Congress, told of his experiences with this reputation as a lawless nation that lynching has given to the United States. "Personally, I have myself seen our civilization sneered at in Europe, in South America and in Mexico. Even in Turkey, I heard of a lecture delivered by a Turk, who displayed pictures of American lynchings to show that America was not a civilized nation." The honour of the United States is stained, and her pretensions to moral leadership of the world are laughed at because of lynchings and the apparent equanimity with which the ruthless murder of her own citizens is viewed by the Government of the United States. Passage and enforcement

of adequate federal legislation against lynching would
be an effective answer to such ridicule of the United
States.

A federal anti-lynching law would aid those who are
battling valiantly against mob-rule where that dangerous practice is widespread and strongly entrenched.
With juries drawn from a wider area, and with judges
who are not dependent upon the votes of lynchers and
their sympathizers for re-election, there would be greater
likelihood of convictions in states where there is little
effective sentiment for suppression of lynching and
where intimidation of courts has destroyed respect for
state courts so far as punishment for lynching of Negroes is concerned, and most of that respect when whites
are the victims. During the debate in Congress on the
Dyer Bill in 1922 the statement was frequently made
by Southern congressmen of both houses that there was
no necessity for federal action, as the states were amply
able to stop lynching. Let us see from the records how
true this has been.

In 1925 there were eighteen lynchings. Six of the
victims were taken from sheriffs or other peace officers
in Southern states, four in Mississippi, and one each in
Arkansas and Florida. Two victims were taken from
jails and lynched, Missouri and Virginia each staging
an episode of this character. One victim, in Mississippi,
was taken from the court-house itself where a jury had
just acquitted him on a charge of murder. Another vic-

tim was lynched after a mob in Georgia had broken into the state insane asylum to obtain possession of the insane man.

In 1926 there were thirty-four lynchings. Eight of the victims were taken from officers of the law, nine were lynched after mobs had broken into jail to obtain them, two were slain in jail by mobs, and one victim in Texas was lynched by officers themselves. Five victims were taken by mobs from officers of the law in Florida, two in Arkansas, and one in Kentucky. Of the nine cases where victims were taken from jails and lynched, three occurred in South Carolina, two in Florida, and one each in Georgia, Louisiana, Mississippi, and Tennessee. One victim was slain in jail by a mob in Mississippi and one in Virginia.

In 1927, of the eighteen victims of mobs, eight were taken from peace officers (Mississippi 3; Arkansas 2; Florida, Texas, and Tennessee one each); four were taken from jails (one each in Kentucky, Mississippi, Missouri, and Tennessee); one was lynched "after he had escaped from policemen" in North Carolina; and in California one was lynched by fellow prisoners.

To summarize, ten of eighteen victims of mobs in 1925, twenty of thirty-four in 1926, and fourteen of eighteen in 1927 were taken from officers, jails, court-houses, and an insane asylum and lynched—forty-four lynchings, out of a total of seventy, where officers of the states were directly responsible. The most optimistic

would find difficulty in terming such a record indicative
of "equal protection of the law"—where the states,
through their agents, were responsible for *not* affording
equal protection of their laws in 62.8 per cent of the
lynchings.

Nor is the record of the courts and grand juries much
better, though indictments and convictions, compared
with previous years, are more frequent. According to
Monroe N. Work of Tuskegee Institute, in the *World
Almanac* for 1927 and 1928, there were seven lynchings
where indictments and convictions followed in 1925 and
1926—during which two years the National Association
for the Advancement of Colored People records fifty-
two lynchings. Mr. Work reports in the seven cases
seventy-five indictments, of which thirty were followed
by convictions. The sentences imposed by the courts
upon these thirty lynchers were as follows: five were
given suspended sentences, one was given thirty days
in jail, and fifteen were sentenced to prison terms ranging from six to eight years—all these in 1925; in 1926
one lyncher was sentenced to life imprisonment and
eight to terms ranging from four to twenty years for
lynching a white man in Georgia.

Against this discouraging picture, encouraging only
by comparison with previous years, should be set in
fairness the record of lynchings prevented. Mr. Work
reports that in 1925 there were thirty-nine such instances, seven in the North and thirty-two in the South.

Action taken consisted of removal of the prisoners, augmenting the guard, or using armed force to repel the lynchers, of which there were thirteen cases. In 1926 thirty-three lynchings were averted, four in Northern and twenty-nine in Southern states.

Federal action may be necessitated by the aftermath of the Ku Klux Klan. Though the peak of this movement seems to have passed, the racial and religious hatred and bigotry that it stirred up and the organization of the most intolerant, criminal, and dangerous elements of various communities will undoubtedly make themselves felt for many years to come. During the debate in Congress of the Dyer Bill in 1922 the constructive criticism was made that the measure became effective only when the victim was killed. This led to the insertion throughout the bill, in addition to the words "for the purpose of depriving any person of his life," the words "or doing him physical injury." The Klan and the spirit it represents have led to situations of virtual armed camps in states like Alabama, where hundreds of men and women, white and Negro, have been lynched, flogged, mutilated, tarred and feathered, and otherwise maltreated by mobs. The Birmingham *News* in 1927 repeatedly declared, as did other newspapers, such as the Montgomery *Advertiser*, that the situation had grown so serious from such outrages that they "constitute the gravest menace now known to this country. Anarchy is anarchy no matter where it raises its head." As the federal government was obliged after the Civil War to drive the Klan and those who adopted Klan methods out of existence, there may come the necessity of similar action to save the lives of its citizens, white and coloured, during these later years.

Though notable progress has been made during recent years against mob-law, the menace to the United States is yet so serious that it is almost impossible to speak in too strong terms regarding it. Perhaps even the most backward states of the present time may be able to find a means of checking the mob. If they do not, it seems inevitable that federal action will be imperative to save these states from themselves and to save the more orderly sections of the country from contamination. Whether that federal action, if it comes, takes the form of a law or a constitutional amendment also remains to be seen.

Lynching—rule by rope and faggot and tar-bucket instead of by orderly and civilized processes—has for too long been a curse to America and an affront to decency and humanity. Against it is needed a larger, more active, more valiant, and more articulate public opinion to restore sanity, truth, and the reign of law. If that organized opinion and action are not forthcoming, sad and terrible days, not only for the lynching states, but for all of America, seem inevitable.

A STATEMENT OF FACT

===

THERE have been lynched in the United States 4951 persons in the forty-six years beginning in 1882 and extending through 1927. Of the victims 3513 were Negroes and 1438 whites. Ninety-two were women—sixteen of them white and seventy-six coloured. Mississippi leads in this exhibition of masculine chivalry, with sixteen women victims; Texas is second with twelve; Alabama and Arkansas are tied for third place with nine each; Georgia follows with eight; Tennessee and South Carolina mobs have bravely murdered seven women each; Kentucky and Louisiana five each, Florida and Oklahoma three each; Missouri and North Carolina two each; and Nebraska, Virginia, and Wyoming one each. Three of the twelve Texas victims were a mother and her two young daughters killed by a mob, in 1918, when they "threatened a white man." Thus was white civilization maintained!

Lynchings were not considered sufficiently important for recording prior to 1882, when the Chicago *Tribune* included in its summary of the year's crimes, disasters, and other phenomena the mob murders of that year. The first scientific and exhaustive study of lynching was that made by Professor James Elbert Cutler of Yale University and Wellesley College. *Lynch-Law* was published in 1905 and covered the years from 1882 through 1903. Unfortunately the book has long been out of print and is practically unobtainable.

Cutler sought "as a student of society and social phenomena" to determine "from the history the causes for the prevalence of the practice, to determine what the social conditions are under which lynch-law operates, and to test the validity of the arguments which have been advanced in justification of lynching." He took the figures as compiled by the Chicago *Tribune* as a basis for his study. With great care he verified and corrected the *Tribune* data through correspondence, and by comparison with the files of other newspapers, such as the New York *Times* and the New York *Tribune*, and through study of all available magazine articles which had been written upon the subject. Because of the care and thoroughness with which he sifted the facts Cutler's study stands as the most thorough examination yet made of the years 1882–1903.

In 1919 the National Association for the Advancement of Colored People published its exceedingly valuable statistical study, *Thirty Years of Lynching in the United States, 1889–1918.* Competent research-workers employed by the Association spent more than six months in the Congressional Library at Washington searching newspaper files; a vast amount of material gathered over a period of ten years by the Association was examined; and, in brief, every source where authoritative evidence could be gained was consulted. Personal investigations of a number of lynchings had been made by members of the Association's staff, and of others by detectives.

Relying upon under- instead of over-statement, the foreword to *Thirty Years* states that "it is believed that more persons have been lynched than those whose names are given. . . . Only such cases have been included as were authenticated by such evidence as was given credence by a recognized newspaper or confirmed by a responsible investigator."

This great caution causes discrepancies between the figures of Cutler and those of the Association. Cutler for the years beginning in 1889 and extending through 1903 gives a higher total in eleven of the fifteen years, and in three others his figures are the same as those of the Association. As Cutler's study was made twenty years nearer to the period, 1889–1903, and because of the care he exercised, his figures for that period are accepted in the present study. This is especially safe inasmuch as the Association's figures are the *minimum* ones.

As further means of checking the above figures, they were compared with the figures of lynchings in the *World Almanac* (1927), prepared by Monroe N. Work of Tuskegee Institute. These figures, covering the period 1885–1925, are in several instances considerably higher than those of Cutler or the Association, especially during the earlier years. For very recent years they are generally slightly lower than those of the Association.

The tables which follow have been prepared, therefore, by combining Cutler's and the Association's figures and carefully checking them with the *World Almanac* figures to insure maximum accuracy.

Table I gives totals of lynchings by years and by race for the years beginning with 1882 and extending through 1927. The figures for the years up to and including 1903 are taken from Cutler. Unfortunately, he indicated the division by race only on a graph, but he gave the totals by years and by race for the fifteen years he studied. For 1904 and the years following, the figures are taken from *Thirty Years*.

Table II lists the lynchings by states and by race. Only four states of the Union have never been stained by a lynching—Massachusetts, Rhode Island, New Hampshire, and Vermont.

TABLE I

Number of Persons Lynched, by Years and by Race,
1882–1927

Year	Total	Whites	Negroes
1882	114		
1883	134		
1884	211		
1885	184		
1886	138		
1887	122		

TABLE I (*continued*)

Year	Total		Whites		Negroes	
1888	142					
1889	176					
1890	128					
1891	195					
1892	235					
1893	200					
1894	197					
1895	180					
1896	131					
1897	165					
1898	127					
1899	107					
1900	115					
1901	135					
1902	97					
1903	104	(3337) *		(1277) *		(2060) *
1904	86		7		79	
1905	65		5		60	
1906	68		4		64	
1907	62		3		59	
1908	100		8		92	
1909	89		14		75	
1910	90		10		80	
1911	80		8		72	
1912	89		3		86	
1913	86		1		85	
1914	74		5		69	
1915	145		46		99	
1916	72		7		65	
1917	54		2		52	
1918	67		4 .		63	
1919	83		4		79	
1920	65		8		57	
1921	64		6		58	

* Totals by race for years 1882–1903 given by Cutler.

TABLE I (*continued*)

Year	Total	Whites	Negroes
1922	61	7	54
1923	28	2	26
1924	16	0	16
1925	18	0	18
1926	34	5	29
1927	18	2	16
	4951	1438	3513

TABLE II

Number of Persons Lynched, By States and By Race,
1882–1927

State	Total	Whites	Negroes
Alabama	356	52	304
Arizona	31	31	0
Arkansas	313	69	244
California	50	48	2
Colorado	68	64	4
Connecticut	1	1	0
Delaware	1	0	1
Florida	275	28	247
Georgia	549	39	510
Idaho	21	21	0
Illinois	32	13	19
Indiana	52	41	11
Iowa	18	17	1
Kansas	55	36	19
Kentucky	233	79	154
Louisiana	409	62	347
Maine	1	1	0
Maryland	27	2	25
Michigan	8	7	1

TABLE II (*continued*)

State	Total	Whites	Negroes
Minnesota	9	5	4
Mississippi	561	44	517
Missouri	117	51	66
Montana	89	87	2
Nebraska	58	55	3
Nevada	6	6	0
New Jersey	1	0	1
New Mexico	38	35	3
New York	3	2	1
North Carolina	100	20	80
North and South Dakota	35	34	1
Ohio	26	11	15
Oklahoma (Indian Territory)	141	97	44
Oregon	20	19	1
Pennsylvania	8	2	6
South Carolina	174	9	165
Tennessee	268	55	213
Texas	534	164	370
Utah	8	6	2
Virginia	109	24	85
Washington	28	27	1
West Virginia	54	21	33
Wisconsin	6	6	0
Wyoming	41	37	4
Alaska and Places Unknown	16	15	1
Totals	4950	1437	3513

Table III gives the states in numerical order of lynchings. It will be noted at once that the first ten states in which have occurred 3672 or 74.166 per cent of the total of 4951 lynchings for all states are in the far

South. As there were two Souths prior to the Civil War on the question of slavery, so since the war there have been two Souths on lynching and its allied evils. The layer of states of the northern South between the Atlantic Ocean and the Mississippi River, which include North Carolina, Virginia, West Virginia, Maryland, and a part of Kentucky, while geographically Southern, are vastly different from the states of the far South, both in number of lynchings and in the brutality with which lynching is practised. Nearer to the more progressive North, these states have a far less bloody record than those farther south. Georgia and her sister states are concrete examples of Booker Washington's truism that one can keep another in the ditch only by lying down beside him and holding him there. The number of lynchings serves as an excellent index of the backwardness of the far South.

TABLE III

States in Numerical Order of Lynchings, 1882–1927

State	Total	Whites	Negroes
Mississippi	561	44	517
Georgia	549	39	510
Texas	534	164	370
Louisiana	409	62	347
Alabama	356	52	304
Arkansas	313	69	244
Florida	275	28	247
Tennessee	268	55	213

TABLE III (*continued*)

State	Total	Whites	Negroes
Kentucky	233	79	154
South Carolina	174	9	165
Oklahoma (Indian Territory)	141	97	44
Missouri	117	51	66
Virginia	109	24	85
North Carolina	100	20	80
Montana	89	87	2
Colorado	68	64	4
Nebraska	58	55	3
Kansas	55	36	19
West Virginia	54	21	33
Indiana	52	41	11
California	50	48	2
Wyoming	41	37	4
New Mexico	38	35	3
North and South Dakota	35	34	1
Illinois	32	13	19
Arizona	31	31	0
Washington	28	27	1
Maryland	27	2	25
Ohio	26	11	15
Idaho	21	21	0
Oregon	20	19	1
Iowa	18	17	1
Alaska and Places Unknown	16	15	1
Minnesota	9	5	4
Michigan	8	7	1
Pennsylvania	8	2	6
Utah	8	6	2
Nevada	6	6	0
Wisconsin	6	6	0
New York	3	2	1
Connecticut	1	1	0

TABLE III (*continued*)

State	Total	Whites	Negroes
Delaware	1	0	1
Maine	1	1	0
New Jersey	1	0	1
Totals	4951	1438	3513

Table IV will give little satisfaction to "hundred per cent Americans" who attribute all lawlessness to "foreigners." It will be observed from this table that lynchings occur in almost an exact inverse ratio to the number of persons of foreign birth within the states. Only North and South Carolina have a lower percentage of foreign-born than Georgia and Mississippi, but these two latter states have lynched 1110 or 22.4 per cent of the total for the entire country. New York, numbering in its population 26.82 per cent of persons of foreign birth, has had only three lynchings in forty-six years, against 561 in Mississippi during the same period, only four-tenths of one per cent of the inhabitants of the latter state having been born outside of the United States. Connecticut, where 27.29 per cent of those residing within the state are foreign born, has had only one lynching in forty-six years. These examples and others indicate considerable justification for the charge that lynching is wholly an American custom and that the propensity for mob murder is in an exact ratio to the "one hundred percentism" of the regions in which they occur.

TABLE IV

Percentage of Foreign-Born and of Lynchings, By States,
1882–1927

State	Total Population 1920 Census	Foreign-Born	Per cent Foreign-Born	Number Lynch-ings	Per cent of Total
Mississippi	1,790,618	8,019	0.44	561	11.331
Georgia	2,895,832	16,186	0.55	549	11.088
Texas	4,663,228	360,519	7.72	534	10.785
Louisiana	1,798,509	44,871	2.44	409	8.260
Alabama	2,348,174	17,662	0.72	356	7.190
Arkansas	1,752,204	13,975	0.68	313	6.321
Florida	968,470	43,008	4.43	275	5.547
Tennessee	2,337,885	15,478	0.64	268	5.406
Kentucky	2,416,630	30,780	1.24	233	4.706
South Carolina	1,683,724	6,401	0.35	174	3.513
Oklahoma	2,028,283	39,968	1.97	141	2.847
Missouri	3,404,055	186,026	5.46	117	2.363
Virginia	2,309,187	30,785	1.29	109	2.201
North Carolina	2,559,123	7,099	0.27	100	2.019
Montana	548,889	93,620	16.93	89	1.797
Colorado	939,629	116,954	12.44	68	1.373
Nebraska	1,296,372	149,652	11.56	58	1.171
Kansas	1,769,257	110,578	6.21	55	1.110
West Virginia	1,463,701	61,906	4.23	54	1.090
Indiana	2,930,390	150,868	5.15	52	1.050
California	3,426,861	681,662	19.90	50	1.009
Wyoming	194,402	25,255	12.88	41	0.828
New Mexico	360,350	29,077	8.05	38	0.767
Dakotas	1,283,419	213,894	16.67	35	0.706
Illinois	6,485,280	1,206,951	18.61	32	0.646
Arizona	334,162	78,099	23.35	31	0.626
Washington	1,356,621	250,055	18.42	28	0.564
Maryland	1,449,661	102,177	7.03	27	0.544
Ohio	5,759,394	678,697	11.79	26	0.524
Idaho	431,866	38,963	9.03	21	0.424

TABLE IV (*continued*)

State	Total Population 1920 Census	Foreign-Born	Per cent Foreign-Born	Number Lynch-ings	Per cent of Total
Oregon	783,389	102,151	13.02	20	0.403
Iowa	2,404,021	225,647	9.40	18	0.363
Alaska	55,036			16	0.323
Minnesota	2,387,125	486,164	20.36	9	0.181
Michigan	3,668,412	726,635	19.82	8	0.161
Pennsylvania	8,720,017	1,387,850	15.91	8	0.161
Utah	449,396	56,455	12.47	8	0.161
Nevada	77,407	14,802	19.12	6	0.121
Wisconsin	2,632,067	460,128	17.47	6	0.121
New York	10,385,227	2,786,112	26.82	3	0.060
Connecticut	1,380,631	376,513	27.29	1	0.020
Delaware	223,003	19,810	8.88	1	0.020
New Jersey	3,155,900	738,613	23.40	1	0.020
Maine	768,014	107,349	13.93	1	0.020

Table V, giving the homicide rate of the twenty-five American cities with the worst records for 1926, illustrates the disrespect for law and the cheapness of human life in the states where lynchings are most frequent. It will be noted that the first five cities in the table are located in the lower South; that the first twelve are Southern or border cities; that twenty of the twenty-five cities with the highest rates are in or on the border of the South. The homicide rate for the whole country in 1926 was 10.1—thus each city listed in the table staged from one and a half to seven and a half times as many homicides as did the country as a whole.

It may be argued by some of these cities that it is unfair to indict a city on the figures for a single year. The answer lies in the reports of the United States Census Bureau. Thirteen of the fifteen cities with the highest homicide rates in 1923 were Southern or border cities—Memphis, Birmingham, Atlanta, Nashville, Kansas City, Mo., New Orleans, Dallas, Louisville, St. Louis, Kansas City, Kan., Houston, Cincinnati, and Norfolk. In 1924 twelve of the fifteen highest were in the same territory—Memphis, Birmingham, Nashville, Atlanta, Kansas City, Mo., New Orleans, Dallas, Houston, Louisville, Kansas City, Kan., St. Louis, and Cincinnati. In 1925 sixteen of the eighteen cities with the highest homicide rates were Southern or border cities —and for that year no figures were made public for Atlanta, Kansas City, (Missouri), Little Rock, Charleston, and Louisville, at least three of which from the records of other years would probably have been among the leaders.

The relation of lynchings to such homicidal tendencies in these Southern cities may be seen by examining their records for a longer period—the thirteen years from 1913 through 1926. Memphis, leader in the murder rate for many years, is located in Tennessee, but geographically belongs to Arkansas and Mississippi also. Since 1881 there have been 268 lynchings in Tennessee, 313 in Arkansas, and 561 in Mississippi—a

total of 1142 or a yearly average of more than twenty-
five. In Memphis the homicide rate per 100,000 population has been: 1914, 73.8; 1915, 88.2: 1916, not given;
1917, 50.8; 1918, 47.4; 1919, 62.1; 1920, 63.0; 1921,
59.2; 1922, 69.1; 1923, 69.4; 1924, 69.7; 1925, 59.0;
1926, 42.4—a yearly average of 62.4. Even the (for
Memphis) apparently modest record in 1926 of only
42.4 persons of each 100,000 killed by other persons
seems to be an understatement of the facts, according to
Hoffman, for, he says, "the time rate for Memphis was
probably higher, if the facts were completely reported.
The figures represent only deaths from murders actually
taking place in the city of Memphis and not as is cus-
tomary with all other cities combining the murder deaths
of both residents and non-residents."

Alabama has staged 356 lynchings since 1881; Birmingham, its chief city, has had over a period of thirteen years an average homicide rate of 53.4. Atlanta,
capital of the Ku Klux Klan and of the state with the
second worst lynching record (549 in forty-six years),
has had an average murder rate for twelve years of
35.73. (No rate is included for Atlanta for 1926.)
Texas (with 534 lynchings in forty-six years) has had
two of its principal cities, Dallas and Houston, ranking
high for years among the homicide cities. Louisiana
ranks fourth among the lynching states, and New Orleans has occupied approximately the same place in
the list of cities with high homicide rates. Hoffman lists

no Mississippi cities in his annual tables of homicides, the figures evidently not being given for them.

So the story runs. Even some of the cities which are not Southern, but which have high homicide rates have been influenced by the lawlessness that lynchings engender. Hoffman says of Detroit's high rate and those of Memphis, Dallas, and Houston, that "in all these localities, the rates are complicated . . . by a large Negro element, which nearly everywhere shows a higher murder death rate than the white population." Concerning Detroit, the facts show that its high rate is partly due to the circumstance that it was a centre not only of Negro migration, but of Southern white migration as well, over two hundred thousand Southern whites going to Detroit within recent years. At one time, during a period of two years, some ninety per cent of the new policemen added to the Detroit force were from the South. Until checked somewhat, they were about to cause a serious clash through their wanton shooting of Negroes. Another factor that affected Detroit in the years 1925 and 1926 was the considerable strength of the Ku Klux Klan, the Klansmen almost electing their candidate for mayor in 1925.

There is a measure of justification for Hoffman's surmise that the presence of a large number of Negroes may affect the homicide rate of certain cities, for lynching brutalizes all classes. It leads as well to a feeling of desperation and hopelessness, which causes certain

types of Negroes to "shoot it out" when clashes come
with whites, since they are convinced that there is little
likelihood of justice or a fair trial later.

The seriousness of the situation in the cities listed in
Table V can be seen by comparison of their records
with that of Chicago, popularly supposed to be more
given to murder than any other city. In 1925 ten cities,
nine of them Southern or border ones, outranked Chicago; in 1926 twenty-two cities, nineteen of them Southern or border ones, had a higher homicide rate. In
proportion to population there were four and a half
murders in Jacksonville to one in Chicago; almost four
to one in Birmingham, and nearly three to one in Memphis. For thirteen years the average murder rate in
Chicago has been 11.8. "Bloody, murderous" Chicago
—where gangsters use machine-guns instead of revol-
vers—begins to take on the air of a peaceful village
when its homicide rate is compared with the average of
62.8 in Memphis, 53.4 in Birmingham, and 35.73 in
Atlanta.

Since industrial centres and ports attract elements
that are more given to crimes of violence, another interesting comparison is that of cities in Table V with
others with similar conditions in states where lynchings
are not common. Here, for example, are the 1926 homicide rates of a few Northern and Western cities, some
with ports, some with many factories: Bridgeport, Conn.,
5.2; Buffalo, N. Y., 5.9; Fall River, Mass., 2.3; Grand

Rapids, Mich., 1.3; Hartford, Conn., 4.3; Jersey City, N. J., 1.6; Paterson, N. J., 4.2; Philadelphia, 8.6; Boston, 3.9; San Francisco, 8.6; Brockton, Mass., 1.4. Not only have these cities the element attracted by industries and ports (and some have large Negro populations), but almost all of them have large numbers of foreign-born among their population, who, according to the beliefs of the average American, are more given to crimes of violence than "pure" Americans.

TABLE V

Twenty-five American Cities with Highest Homicide Rates for the Year 1926 *

1. Jacksonville, Fla.	75.9
2. Tampa, Fla.	67.6
3. Birmingham, Ala.	58.8
4. Memphis, Tenn.	42.4
5. New Orleans, La.	33.7
6. Kansas City, Mo.	32.3
7. Dallas, Tex.	32.0
8. Charleston, S. C.	29.7
9. Nashville, Tenn.	29.2
10. Mobile, Ala.	28.4
11. Louisville, Ky.	26.7
12. Houston, Tex.	25.8
13. Detroit, Mich.	25.3
14. Sacramento, Cal.	21.8
15. Shreveport, La.	21.8
16. Little Rock, Ark.	21.1
17. Pueblo, Colo.	20.5
18. Kansas City, Kan.	18.8
19. St. Louis, Mo.	18.6
20. Cincinnati, Ohio.	18.2

TABLE V (*continued*)

21.	Winston-Salem, N. C.	18.1
22.	Knoxville, Tenn.	17.2
23.	Chicago, Ill.	16.7
24.	Gary, Ind.	16.1
25.	Macon, Ga.	15.2

* As compiled by Frederick L. Hoffman, LL.D., Consulting Statistician, Prudential Life Insurance Company of America, and published in the *Spectator* of June 2, 1927.

Table V presents, therefore, a situation worthy of sober reflection, not only by the cities concerned, but by the country at large. Even those who hold violent prejudices against the Negro need to realize that there is no contagious disease known to medical science which is more easily transferred than unrestrained lawlessness. Wilful, frequent, and unchecked violence directed against Negroes, the taking of the law into its own hands by the mob, the disregard of the human and civil rights and of the safety of person of any element of the population, spread with alarming speed to similar action against other elements. Alabama is a clear-cut example of this truth. Ruled by the Klan, its governor being a member, there were hundreds of floggings, kidnappings, tarring and featherings, and other outrages in that state in 1927, most of them not of Negroes, but of white men and women. So serious did the situation become that the Birmingham *News* on September 6 declared: "Unless the governor is determined that the whole state shall be turned into a walking arsenal he will act in the matter and act at once. If he fails to act then each citizen of Alabama will be encouraged to go armed to the teeth ready and determined to shoot down these masked and hooded cowards who in the name of 'law-enforcement' mock all law and mock also the peace and dignity of this commonwealth." Alabama's experience, recent events have taught, is not an isolated one. One can better understand from this statement why Birmingham and Mobile have ranked so high among the cities with disgraceful homicide records. Unrestrained brutality by lynchers against black victims inevitably creates a situation where no man, high or low, black or white, is free from the possibility of paying with his life for promiscuous mobbism. It would seem as though so evident a fact would have wrought a change and ended lynching—not to save black victims from lynching, but to save white men and women.

Table VI illustrates as clearly, perhaps, as is possible the effect of emotional, primitive religion upon lynching figures. The connexion between lynching and religion has been discussed. Careful scrutiny of this table will doubtless be an astonishing revelation of the almost exactly parallel curve upwards of lynchings and of the Methodist-Baptist percentage of the total of church members in those states where lynchings have occurred. Where the percentage of Roman Catholics, Congregationalists, Presbyterians, Episcopalians, Unitarians, and other less emotional denominations rises, and of those professing no church allegiance, the number of lynchings decreases.

It is particularly desired that the presentation of such facts may not be construed as attacks upon any one denomination or as absolution from responsibility of any other. The figures are given for their remarkable revelatory character in bearing down upon the problem of lynch-law. To some readers such figures may indicate only a tenuous connexion between primitivism in religion and mobbism. To others the dominance of the Protestant clergy and especially a poorly paid, ignorant, and uneducated clergy such as afflicts most of the rural South will appear responsible in considerable measure, not only for much of the spirit of bigotry which gives birth to lynching, but to many other forms of intolerance as well.

Louisiana and Texas, at first glance, with a lower percentage of Methodists and Baptists than the states round them and with the highest number of persons lynched, would seem to offer contradictory testimony. A little more careful scrutiny reveals that the seeming contradiction does not exist.

Texas had, according to Table VI, 402,874 Roman Catholics. In 1920, however, the United States Census shows that there were in Texas 249,652 Mexicans, most of whom, it may be assumed with reasonable safety, are Catholics. Eliminating these Mexicans, one discovers that

Methodists and Baptists number 69.3 per cent of Texas church membership.

Louisiana, with the lowest percentage of Methodists and Baptists in relation to her total church membership of any of the states with high lynching records, offers an even more striking example. The *World Almanac* for 1927, quoting the figures from the *Official Catholic Directory* for 1926, reveals that there were 331,921 Catholics in the diocese of New Orleans alone. If we subtract this number from the total of Catholics in all of Louisiana shown in the table, 509,910, and by the result thus obtained divide the combined number of Louisiana Methodists and Baptists, we find that Louisiana outside of New Orleans is 55.4 per cent Methodist or Baptist. And scrutiny of the lynching figures discloses that of 168 lynchings in Louisiana since 190 only one has taken place in New Orleans. Other factors of necessity enter into the equation, but it cannot be questioned that an illiterate ministry working with the tools of a primitive, emotional religion does play a not inconsiderable part in the problem of the continued reign of Judge Lynch. It seems entirely safe to assert that much greater headway in the efforts to end lynching would be made if there were considerable augmentation of the number of educated, intelligent Methodist and Baptist ministers of both races now at work in the South.

The population figures in Table VI are from the

TABLE VI

States by Number of Persons Lynched, by Population, by Church Membership, and by Denominations

State	Total Population 1920 Census	Church Members All Denominations	Roman Catholic	Methodist	Baptist	Other Protestants*	Percentage of Methodists and Baptists in Total Church Population*	Total Number of Persons Lynched, 1882–1927
Mississippi	1,790,618	762,977	32,160	226,356	441,293	26,261	87.5	561
Georgia	2,895,832	1,234,132	18,214	387,775	721,140	42,398	89.8	549
Texas	4,663,228	1,784,620	402,874	418,121	646,494	107,323	59.7	534
Louisiana	1,798,509	863,067	509,910	81,273	213,018	23,033	34.09	409
Alabama	2,348,174	1,099,465	37,482	323,400	518,706	35,319	76.59	356
Arkansas	1,752,204	583,209	21,120	176,806	287,349	23,384	79.5	313
Florida	968,470	324,856	24,650	114,821	131,107	23,631	75.7	275
Tennessee	2,337,885	840,133	23,015	286,143	320,442	84,414	72.2	268
Kentucky	2,416,630	967,702	160,185	155,129	367,731	60,576	54.03	233
South Carolina	1,683,724	794,126	72,113	278,854	413,630	64,696	87.2	174
Oklahoma	2,028,283	424,492	47,427	113,202	129,436	34,988	57.1	141
Missouri	3,404,055	1,370,551	445,352	241,751	252,107	139,834	36.03	117
Virginia	2,309,187	949,136	36,671	147,954	456,095	100,424	63.6	109
North Carolina	2,559,123	1,080,723	4,989	338,979	535,299	118,121	80.89	100
Montana	548,889	137,566	78,113	13,873	4,073	24,880	13.04	89
Colorado	939,629	257,977	104,982	38,594	18,548	49,483	22.1	68
Nebraska	1,296,372	440,791	135,537	81,879	19,643	124,739	23.02	58
Kansas	1,769,257	610,347	128,948	151,348	60,383	100,190	34.69	55
West Virginia	1,463,701	427,865	60,337	154,519	78,679	35,776	54.5	54

Indiana	2,930,390	1,777,341	272,288	271,596	85,786	132,722	20.1	52
California	3,426,861	893,366	494,539	96,818	39,570	129,582	15.2	50
Wyoming	194,402	39,505	12,801	4,293	1,841	9,259	15.5	41
New Mexico	360,350	209,809	177,727	11,505	6,721	5,976	8.68	38
Dakotas	1,283,419	424,894	167,972	34,908	15,120	172,944	11.7	35
Illinois	6,485,280	2,522,373	1,171,381	287,931	170,452	412,043	18.17	32
Arizona	334,162	117,014	84,742	5,651	2,972	7,210	7.36	31
Washington	1,356,621	283,709	97,418	40,020	17,738	77,497	20.3	28
Maryland	1,449,661	602,587	219,530	161,287	44,055	108,303	34.07	27
Ohio	5,759,394	2,291,793	843,856	399,045	105,753	404,187	22.02	26
Idaho	431,866	135,386	17,947	11,373	5,682	12,257	12.59	21
Oregon	783,389	179,468	49,728	30,381	15,635	34,557	25.6	20
Iowa	2,404,021	937,334	262,513	199,036	44,939	209,053	26.02	18
Minnesota	2,387,125	931,388	415,664	59,576	28,156	346,577	9.4	9
Michigan	3,668,412	1,181,431	572,117	144,094	49,766	235,984	16.4	8
Pennsylvania	8,720,017	4,114,527	1,830,532	427,509	194,262	1,125,104	15.1	8
Utah	449,396	280,848	10,000	1,848	1,305	5,339	1.1	8
Nevada	77,407	16,145	8,742	777	356	2,413	7.01	6
Wisconsin	2,632,067	1,162,032	594,836	63,331	20,425	380,689	7.2	6
New York	10,385,227	4,315,404	2,745,552	328,250	182,443	669,454	11.8	3
Connecticut	1,380,631	724,692	483,834	36,181	26,243	140,072	8.6	1
Delaware	223,003	86,524	30,183	37,521	3,651	11,793	47.5	1
Maine	768,014	258,293	118,530	22,551	35,492	30,077	22.7	1
New Jersey	3,155,900	1,337,983	790,764	131,211	80,918	240,888	15.8	1

* Presbyterian, Congregationalist, Protestant Episcopal, Unitarian, Lutheran, and Reformed.

United States Census of 1920; the figures of church membership are taken from the 1927 *World Almanac.*

Table VI should also be studied in connexion with Table VII, which gives by race, by states, and by five-year periods the number of persons lynched from 1881 through 1927. A number of states with a low Methodist-Baptist percentage which occupy relatively high positions among the lynching states are located in the West and but recently have passed through the pioneer stage where there were few courts of law. Montana is an example of this class of states. It occupies in Table VI fifteenth place among the lynching states, with a total of eighty-nine. Table VII reveals, however, that eighty-five of the eighty-nine lynchings occurred in the period between 1882 and 1903, when the state was first being generally opened up, and that only four lynchings have taken place in Montana during the past twenty-four years.

Colorado is another case in point. Sixty-eight lynchings give it sixteenth place among the lynching states —but sixty-four of these lynchings occurred prior to 1904 and only four since 1903. Fifty-six of the fifty-eight lynchings in Nebraska were staged prior to 1904; fifty-one of the fifty-five in Kansas; forty-one of the forty-nine in California; thirty-seven of the forty-one in Wyoming; thirty-four of the thirty-eight in New Mexico; all of the thirty-five in the Dakotas; all of the thirty-one in Arizona; twenty-six of the twenty-eight in Washington; nineteen of the twenty-one in Idaho; six of the nine in Minnesota; seven of the eight in Utah; five of the six in Nevada; and all six in Wisconsin. When these figures are compared with the records of such states as Mississippi, Georgia, Texas, Louisiana, Arkansas, South Carolina, and other states with continuously bad records for lynching, it seems that the connexion between lynching and religion in the Southern and border states is closer than would appear on the surface.

Table VII indicates the sore spots of lynching in the United States, where lynching has continued despite the puncturing of the myth that this crime is necessary for the protection of white womanhood and where there is no possible justification such as existed in the early days of frontier life. The picture presented in this fashion is clear enough to necessitate no verbal elaboration.

The Alleged Causes of Lynching

There was once a general conviction that most if not all lynchings were in expiation of sex crimes committed by Negroes upon white women. Within the past decade, however, that belief has been so thoroughly shown to be without foundation in fact that no reasonably well-informed or intelligent person is longer led astray by

it. As we have already seen, charges of rape or attempted rape have been industriously circulated by
lynchers not only for the purpose of avoiding punishment for their crime but to gain approval of their action. Cutler, a careful student, found that during the
period of twenty-two years which he studied, 1882–
1903, of 2060 Negroes lynched only 707 were *charged*
with "the crime of rape, either attempted, alleged, or
actually committed." [1] Charges of murder ranked first,
with 783 lynchings; rape was second; "minor offenses"
caused the lynching of 208 Negroes; arson took fourth
place among alleged causes with 104 victims; theft
came fifth with 101; and among other alleged causes
ninety Negroes were lynched during that period for
"unknown reasons."

*Thirty Years of Lynching in the United States, 1889–
1918,* published by the National Association for the
Advancement of Colored People, reveals that of 2522
Negroes lynched during that period 900, or 35.8 per
cent were charged with murder; 477, or 19.0 per cent,
with rape; 303, or 12.0 per cent, died at the hands of
mobs for "miscellaneous crimes"; 253, or 9.5 per
cent, were charged with "crimes against the person";
which included such "offences" as striking or talking
back to a white man; 237, or 9.4 per cent, were charged
with attacks upon women, among which were placed

[1] *Lynch-Law,* p. 178.

"all cases in which press accounts state that attacks upon women were made, but in which it was not clear whether rape was alleged to have been consummated or attempted." Of the remaining 352 Negro victims, 210, or 8.3 per cent, were charged with crimes against property, and 142, or 5.6 per cent, were placed in the classification of "absence of crime," which included such things as "testifying against whites," "suing whites," "wrong man lynched," "race prejudice," and such "offences."

It may be assumed with full safety that in every case where there was the slightest intimation or suspicion of rape or attempted rape upon a white woman newspaper accounts would mention the fact. For the purpose of giving the lynchers every benefit of the doubt, let us include the 237 Negroes (9.4 per cent) lynched for "attacks upon women" with the 477 lynched for alleged rape. The greatest possible total is therefore 714 Negroes who can be charged with rape, alleged rape, attempted rape, suspicion of rape, or of offences of any other nature, no matter how slight, against a white woman, out of a total of 2522 lynched for all offences. The maximum therefore would be 28.3 per cent, or less than one in three victims. If we confine ourselves to cases where Negroes were specifically charged with rape, the number of such accusations falls to slightly less than one in five.

TABLE VII

*Number of Persons Lynched, by States, by Race, and by
Periods, 1882–1927*

	1882–1903	1904–1908	1909–1913	1914–1918	1919–1923	1924–1927	Totals
Alabama							
White	46	0	2	0	4	0	52
Negro	198	29	35	24	17	1	304
Total	244	29	37	24	21	1	356
Arizona							
White	28	0	0	3	0	0	31
Negro	0	0	0	0	0	0	0
Total	28	0	0	3	0	0	31
Arkansas							
White	61	1	1	5	1	0	69
Negro	139	31	24	20	23	7	244
Total	200	32	25	25	24	7	313
California							
White	41	2	0	1	3	1	48
Negro	0	1	1	0	0	0	2
Total	41	3	1	1	3	1	50
Colorado							
White	61	1	0	0	2	0	64
Negro	3	0	0	1	0	0	4
Total	64	1	0	1	2	0	68
Connecticut							
White	1	0	0	0	0	0	1
Negro	0	0	0	0	0	0	0
Total	1	0	0	0	0	0	1
Delaware							
White	0	0	0	0	0	0	0
Negro	1	0	0	0	0	0	1
Total	1	0	0	0	0	0	1
Florida							
White	19	2	2	3	1	1	28
Negro	115	13	44	23	34	18	247
Total	134	15	46	26	35	19	275

TABLE VII (*continued*)

	1882–1903	1904–1908	1909–1913	1914–1918	1919–1923	1924–1927	*Totals*
Georgia							
White	28	3	3	3	0	2	39
Negro	241	52	75	79	58	5	510
Total	269	55	78	82	58	7	549
Idaho							
White	19	1	1	0	0	0	21
Negro	0	0	0	0	0	0	0
Total	19	1	1	0	0	0	21
Illinois							
White	11	0	0	2	0	0	13
Negro	10	2	4	2	0	1	19
Total	21	2	4	4	0	1	32
Indiana							
White	41	0	0	0	0	0	41
Negro	11	0	0	0	0	0	11
Total	52	0	0	0	0	0	52
Iowa							
White	16	1	0	0	0	0	17
Negro	0	0	0	1	0	0	1
Total	16	1	0	1	0	0	18
Kansas							
White	34	0	0	1	1	0	36
Negro	17	0	1	0	1	0	19
Total	51	0	1	1	2	0	55
Kentucky							
White	64	5	5	5	0	0	79
Negro	103	14	11	20	2	4	154
Total	167	19	16	25	2	4	233
Louisiana							
White	53	3	2	0	4	0	62
Negro	232	29	31	36	15	4	347
Total	285	32	33	36	19	4	409
Maine							
White	0	1	0	0	0	0	1
Negro	0	0	0	0	0	0	0
Total	0	1	0	0	0	0	1

TABLE VII (*continued*)

	1882–1903	1904–1908	1909–1913	1914–1918	1919–1923	1924–1927	Totals
Maryland							
White	2	0	0	0	0	0	2
Negro	18	4	3	0	0	0	25
Total	20	4	3	0	0	0	27
Michigan							
White	7	0	0	0	0	0	7
Negro	1	0	0	0	0	0	1
Total	8	0	0	0	0	0	8
Minnesota							
White	5	0	0	0	0	0	5
Negro	1	0	0	0	3	0	4
Total	6	0	0	0	3	0	9
Mississippi							
White	40	0	1	1	1	1	44
Negro	294	76	44	43	44	16	517
Total	334	76	45	44	45	17	561
Missouri							
White	49	0	1	0	1	0	51
Negro	42	4	6	7	4	3	66
Total	91	4	7	7	5	3	117
Montana							
White	84	0	1	1	1	0	87
Negro	1	0	1	0	0	0	2
Total	85	0	2	1	1	0	89
Nebraska							
White	54	0	1	0	0	0	55
Negro	2	0	0	0	1	0	3
Total	56	0	1	0	1	0	58
Nevada							
White	5	1	0	0	0	0	6
Negro	0	0	0	0	0	0	0
Total	5	1	0	0	0	0	6
New Jersey							
White	0	0	0	0	0	0	0
Negro	1	0	0	0	0	0	1
Total	1	0	0	0	0	0	1

TABLE VII (*continued*)

	1882–1903	1904–1908	1909–1913	1914–1918	1919–1923	1924–1927	Totals
New Mexico							
White	33	0	0	1	0	1	35
Negro	1	2	0	0	0	0	3
Total	34	2	0	1	0	1	38
New York							
White	1	0	0	1	0	0	2
Negro	1	0	0	0	0	0	1
Total	2	0	0	1	0	0	3
North Carolina							
White	16	1	0	3	0	0	20
Negro	48	7	3	9	12	1	80
Total	64	8	3	2	12	1	100
North and South Dakota							
White	34	0	0	0	0	0	34
Negro	1	0	0	0	0	0	1
Total	35	0	0	0	0	0	35
Ohio							
White	10	0	1	0	0	0	11
Negro	11	1	2	0	1	0	15
Total	21	1	3	0	1	0	26
Oklahoma							
White	88	0	5	1	3	0	97
Negro	7	5	16	11	5	0	44
Total	95	5	21	12	8	0	141
Oregon							
White	18	0	0	1	0	0	19
Negro	1	0	0	0	0	0	1
Total	19	0	0	1	0	0	20
Pennsylvania							
White	2	0	0	0	0	0	2
Negro	5	0	1	0	0	0	6
Total	7	0	1	0	0	0	8

TABLE VII (*continued*)

	1882–1903	1904–1908	1909–1913	1914–1918	1919–1923	1924–1927	Totals
South Carolina							
White	8	1	0	0	0	0	9
Negro	109	14	18	10	10	4	165
Total	117	15	18	10	10	4	174
Tennessee							
White	49	1	1	0	3	1	55
Negro	150	17	22	17	2	5	213
Total	199	18	23	17	5	6	268
Texas							
White	125	2	4	30	2	1	164
Negro	199	45	46	39	35	6	370
Total	324	47	50	69	37	7	534
Utah							
White	6	0	0	0	0	0	6
Negro	1	0	0	0	0	1	2
Total	7	0	0	0	0	1	8
Virginia							
White	21	2	1	0	0	0	24
Negro	70	4	2	4	3	2	85
Total	91	6	3	4	3	2	109
Washington							
White	26	0	0	0	1	0	27
Negro	0	0	0	1	0	0	1
Total	26	0	0	1	1	0	28
West Virginia							
White	19	0	1	0	1	0	21
Negro	27	0	3	1	2	0	33
Total	46	0	4	1	3	0	54
Wisconsin							
White	6	0	0	0	0	0	6
Negro	0	0	0	0	0	0	0
Total	6	0	0	0	0	0	6

TABLE VII (*continued*)

	1882–1903	1904–1908	1909–1913	1914–1918	1919–1923	1924–1927	Totals
Wyoming							
White	37	0	0	0	0	0	37
Negro	0	2	1	1	0	0	4
Total	37	2	1	1	0	0	41
Alaska and Places Unknown							
White	14	1	0	0	0	0	15
Negro	0	0	0	1	0	0	1
Total	14	1	0	1	0	0	16

Note: It will be observed in Tables II, III, IV, VI, and VII that four states—New Hampshire, Massachusetts, Rhode Island, and Vermont—are not listed. No lynchings have occurred in these states.

It would, however, be most unsafe to assume that lynchers, though murderers, are and always have been of unquestioned veracity. James Weldon Johnson in *Current History* (January 1924) succinctly warns students of the question on this point: "It should be borne in mind that a mob's accusation is not by any means equivalent to conviction, or even to an indictment for crime by a regularly constituted jury. In fact, in a number of cases in which investigators were sent to the scene of lynchings by the National Association for the Advancement of Colored People, their reports showed that the victim's guilt had not only not been proved, but that he was actually innocent of the crime charged." The writer goes on to dispose of the industriously circulated impression that the Negro is addicted to sex crimes more than any other race. He points out that in the five-year period between 1914 and 1918 of 264 Negroes lynched only twenty-eight were charged with rape. He contrasts this record with that of New York County, which is only a part of New York City, and finds "that in the single year 1917 there were 230 persons indicted for rape, of whom thirty-seven were indicted for rape in the first degree. That is, in just a part of New York City, nine more persons were indicted for rape in the first degree than there were Negroes lynched on the charge of rape throughout the entire United States in a five-year period. Not one of the thirty-seven persons indicted in New York County was a Negro."

Johnson adds the obvious but all too often ignored fact "that the evidence required by the Grand Jury of New York County to indict a person on the charge of rape must be more conclusive than the evidence required by or submitted to a lynching mob. The New York Grand Jury requires corroboration, direct or circumstantial; the unsupported word of a woman is not sufficient. The mob does not even require, in most cases, that the woman be certain as to the identity of the accused man."

Another effective answer to those who invariably connect lynchings with charges of rape is that ninety-two women have been lynched by American mobs since 1881, a number of them done to death with extreme cruelty.

Study of the lynchings and alleged causes given for those during the period from 1918 through 1927 discloses an interesting situation as lynchers meet the growing sentiment, North and South, against lynching. Southern communities, even when isolated, have grown increasingly sensitive to criticism and condemnation under the continued outcry against the barbarity. Explosion of the myth that rape causes lynching, and the tendency to investigation of the facts, both by organizations interested in the subject, such as the National Association for the Advancement of Colored People, which has done the most notable and extensive work in this field, and by newspapers, have tended to cause less frequent and brazen assignment of petty offences as reasons for mob murders.

There has been noted, too, a growing scepticism regarding charges by women of rape or attempted rape. Within recent years there have been several cases where investigation proved that women have raised charges of rape by Negroes to cover their own misdeeds or when hysterical, or excited by newspaper or other reports of alleged attacks upon other women. In New Jersey in 1927, for example, a man was killed while riding in his automobile with his wife, who declared to the police that two Negro hold-up men had murdered him as he sought to protect her. Shortly afterwards the woman and her lover were indicted, convicted, and sentenced to prison for the murder.

In June 1927, at Hickory Grove, South Carolina, a young married woman of twenty claimed that "a tall, yellow Negro" had attempted to assault her as she was picking blackberries. The Columbia, South Carolina *Record* reported that York County "was stirred to a boiling point again today . . . a crowd of several hundred men . . . are searching the countryside in an effort to find the Negro . . . feeling running high." The Columbia *State* supplied the sequel the following day: "After spending yesterday in the grip of a feverish excitement that spread to all parts of York County, resulting from the assertion of a young married woman that an attempt at criminal assault had been made on her by a strange Negro, the Hickory Grove community today returned to its accustomed calm. . . . The opinion, beginning yesterday morning and gaining headway in the afternoon, that there was absolutely nothing to the assault story, had today crystallized into settled conviction, the general opinion appears to be that the assault story had as its excuse . . . no hallucination or an hysterical imagination. It must be accounted for on other grounds . . . ! The Hickory Grove Hoax . . . has passed into history." A prominent South Carolina attorney adds significantly in a letter to the writer: "One has to read between the lines to gather why it is so referred to."

Ray Stannard Baker in *Following the Color Line* relates how the notorious Atlanta riot of 1906 was largely caused by yellow journalism in the reporting in lurid head-lines of cases of alleged criminal assault— most of which were found later to be wholly without foundation in fact. The Washington race riot of 1919 was, similarly, caused in large measure by the newspaper featuring of seven cases of alleged assault. *Subsequent investigation revealed that four of the seven had been attacks on colored women by white men, and that one of the remaining three cases was that of a woman who, behind in her payments on a fur coat, sought to gain public sympathy and thus prevent impending seizure of the coat.*

Revelations such as these have done much within recent years towards creation of greater scepticism on the part of intelligent newspaper editors and the general public. With this has come a growing courage and articulateness, notably among Southern white women, in repudiating the imputation that lynching is necessary for the protection of white women. These and other salutary developments have come in the wake of organized, persistent, and scientific campaigns against Judge Lynch, notably by the National Association for the Advancement of Colored People and the Interracial Commission. The most significant results of such efforts have been a gratifying growth of public sentiment against lynching and a downward trend of the number of victims. Against these encouraging signs are balanced greater efforts to conceal lynchings in remote districts of the South, and a tendency falsely to allege grave offences instead of brazenly proclaiming lynching for exceedingly petty offences.

A survey of lynching and the causes assigned for lynchings since 1918 will indicate this changing psychology. In 1919 eighty-three persons were lynched, of which number twenty-seven, or 32.5 per cent, were accused of murder. Fourteen, or 16.8 per cent, of the victims were charged with rape, while five others were accused of attempted rape. Combining the two latter groups, nineteen, or but 22.8 per cent, of the total of eighty-three were charged with sex offences. Two other Negroes were lynched in 1919 for "intimacy with white women," but these victims, even if guilty, could hardly be charged with rape or attempted rape.

Twenty-four of the sixty-five persons lynched in 1920, or 36.9 per cent, were charged with murder; fifteen, or 23.0 per cent, were accused of attacks on women. There were six victims in Florida when a prosperous, respected Negro physician, a duly qualified voter, sought to vote in the presidential election of that year. Among other causes assigned for the murder of the remaining twenty victims of 1920 were "jumping labour contract," "insanity," and "assaulting white man."

In 1921 charges of attacks upon women as justification of lynchings exceeded in number those for murder. Nineteen or 29.6 per cent of the year's total of sixty-

four were charged with attacks, one was accused of attempted assault, and eighteen, or 28.1 per cent, were
charged with murder.

Judge Lynch claimed sixty-one victims in 1922, of
whom twenty (32.7 per cent) were charged with assault); three (4.9 per cent) with attempted assault;
nine (14.7 per cent) with murder; and the remainder
with charges ranging from "improper relations with
white woman" to "a Fourth of July celebration."

Seven of twenty-eight persons lynched in 1923, or
exactly 25.0 per cent, were charged with sex offences.
Three were killed by mobs for murder, one for "as-
sociating with white women," another for "accusing
white men of stealing," another for "frightening children," and one for "remaining in town where Negroes
were not allowed"; and a colored woman in Mississippi was lynched by a mob "in search of another."

In 1924 the annual toll of victims dropped sharply to
sixteen, of whom five (31.2 per cent) were charged with
rape; four (25.0 per cent) with attempted rape; and
three (18.7 per cent) with murder.

Eighteen persons were lynched in 1925, five (27.7
per cent) being accused of rape, and eight (44.4 per
cent) of murder. Of the latter, one was seized at Clarks-
dale, Mississippi, and lynched as he left the court-
house where a jury had acquitted him of the murder
with which he was charged; two others were insane.

The tendency noted during the years 1921 onward

to ascribe rape and more serious offences was most noticeable during the time that the Dyer Anti-Lynching Bill was pending in the national Congress.

Out of thirty-four victims in 1926 eight (23.5 per cent) were charged with rape; sixteen (47.0 per cent) with murder, of whom one had been acquitted and three others seemed likely to be freed; one was accused of "suspicion in connection with an attack upon a white woman."

Four (27.2 per cent) of eighteen victims in 1927 were accused of attacks upon women; one (5.5 per cent) with attempted attack; seven (38.8 per cent) with murder.

To summarize, within the last nine years, 1919–27, there was a total of 387 lynchings, an average per year of forty-three. One hundred and fifteen of the victims, or 29.7 per cent, were charged with murder; ninety-seven, or 25.06 per cent, were accused of rape; and fifteen, or 3.87 per cent, with attempted rape. Even though the two latter classes are combined to include every case where a crime was connected with sex, the result is only 29.93 per cent. Thus even when the statements of the mobs, who have acted as judge, jury, and executioner and destroyed most of the evidence, are accepted, less than one in three of nearly four hundred victims have even been accused of sex crimes.

The most prejudice-ridden lyncher would not contend that a Negro accused of murder would not be fairly

tried and executed by the law if he was guilty. Yet it is
seen that between 1889 and 1918 exactly 900, or 35.8
per cent, of 2522 Negroes lynched were charged with
murder; 115 or 387 victims since 1918 were accused
of the same crime. Accusations of murder, like those
of rape, have been fairly constant in proportion to the
total number of lynchings during all the recorded history of lynching. Thus, on the sole ground of efficiency,
the figures demonstrate the failure of lynching to end
the very crimes against which its apologists declare it
to be aimed. The United States, boastful of its modernity and ruthless discarding of archaic systems, has
clung to this system which, irrespective of its sadism,
its slaughter of women and innocent victims, its de-
humanizing brutality, has consistently failed in the
very objects for which it has been perpetuated and
defended.

Summary

1. Four thousand nine hundred and fifty-one persons,
an annual average of 107.6, were lynched during the
forty-six years 1882–1927, in forty-four states and
Alaska. Of that number 1438 were white and 3513
colored. Seventy-six Negro women and sixteen white
women were included among the victims.

2. There has been a notable annual decrease in the
number of persons lynched, with occasional exceptions,
since the turn of the century. The average per year dur-

ing the past ten years, 1918–27, dropped to 45.4,
against an average of 87.9 during 1908–17, and of 96.6
for 1898–1907.

3. One border state, Kentucky, and nine states of the
far South—Mississippi, Georgia, Texas, Louisiana,
Alabama, Arkansas, Florida, Tennessee, and South
Carolina—have between them staged slightly less than
three-fourths—74.166 per cent—of all lynchings
within the past forty-six years.

4. The curve of lynchings has followed almost exactly a trend diametrically opposite to the percentage
of foreign-born in the total populations of various
states.

5. The homicide rate per hundred thousand inhabitants of cities in states where most lynchings have occurred follows roughly the same curves as lynching in
these states and sections.

6. Lynchings generally are numerous or few in proportion to the percentage of Methodists and Baptists in
the total church membership of the various states; less
exactly there appears a relationship between the percentage of church members in the total population and
that of lynchings. Lynchings appear to decrease in
somewhat inverse proportion to the number of communicants of the less emotional and primitive denominations.

7. The once generally held belief that most if not all
lynchings were connected with sex crimes is not borne

out by the facts, or even by the causes of lynchings alleged by the mobs themselves.

8. Northern and Western states have almost completely abandoned lynching with the passing of frontier conditions. Only the Southern states, and especially those of the far South, more or less regularly resort to the practice.

BIBLIOGRAPHY

BEARD, CHARLES A. and MARY R.: *The Rise of American Civilization* (2 vols.). New York, 1927

BIGHAM, J. A. (editor): *Select Discussions of Race Problems* (No. 20 of the Atlanta University Publications). Atlanta, Georgia, 1916

BOAS, FRANZ: *The Mind of Primitive Man.* New York, 1911

BOGART, ERNEST LUDLOW: *Economic History of the United States* (4th revised edition). New York, 1922

BRAWLEY, BENJAMIN: *A Social History of the American Negro.* New York, 1921

BRIGHAM, C. C.: *Study of American Intelligence.*

BROWNE, LEWIS: *This Believing World.* New York, 1926

COLLINS, WINFIELD H.: *The Truth About Lynching and the Negro in the South.* New York, 1918

CUTLER, JAMES ELBERT: *Lynch-Law.* New York, 1905

DORSEY, GEORGE A.: *Why We Behave Like Human Beings.* New York, 1925

— "Race and Civilization," chapter x in *Whither Mankind,* edited by Charles A. Beard. New York, 1928

DuBois, W. E. B.: *The Negro.* New York, 1915

Evans, Maurice S.: *Black and White in the Southern States.* New York, 1915

Finot, Jean: *Race Prejudice.* New York, 1907

Grant, Madison: *The Passing of the Great Race.* New York, 1916

Gregory, J. W.: *The Menace of Colour.* London, 1925

Hankins, Frank H.: *The Racial Basis of Civilization.* New York, 1926

Hays, Arthur Garfield: *Let Freedom Ring.* New York, 1928

Hertz, Friedrich: *Race and Civilization.* New York, 1928

Hurd, John C.: *The Law of Freedom and Bondage* (2 vols.). Boston, 1858–62

James, William: *Varieties of Religious Experience.*

Johnson, James Weldon: *Self-Determining Haiti.* New York, 1920

Kelsey, Carl: *The Physical Basis of Society* (revised edition). New York, 1928

Kroeber, A. L.: *Anthropology.* New York, 1923

Langdon-Davies, John: *The New Age of Faith.* New York, 1925

Leys, Norman: *Kenya.* London, 1925

Martin, Everett Dean: *The Behavior of Crowds.* New York, 1920

Mecklin, John Moffatt: *Democracy and Race Friction.* New York, 1914

Merriam, George S.: *The Negro and the Nation.* New York, 1906

Miller, Herbert Adolphus: *Races, Nations and Classes.* Philadelphia, 1924

Mims, Edwin: *The Advancing South.* Garden City, 1926

Morel, E. D.: *The Black Man's Burden.* New York, 1920

Olivier, Lord: *The Anatomy of African Misery.* London, 1927

OLMSTEAD, FREDERICK LAW: *A Journey in the Seaboard Slave States in the Years 1853–1854* (revised edition; first published 1856). New York, 1904

PROCEEDINGS OF THE NATIONAL NEGRO CONFERENCE (New York, May 31 and June 1, 1909) (Out of print)

REUTER, EDWARD BYRON: *The Mulatto in the United States.* Boston, 1918

ROBERTSON, WILLIAM J.: *The Changing South.* New York, 1927

ROBINSON, JAMES HARVEY: *The Mind in the Making.* New York, 1921

SELIGMAN, EDWIN R. A.: *Principles of Economics.* New York, 1909 (Chap. XI on slavery.)

SIEGFRIED, ANDRÉ: *America Comes of Age.* New York, 1927

SHIPLEY, MAYNARD: *The War on Modern Science.* New York, 1927

SKAGGS, WILLIAM H.: *The Southern Oligarchy.* New York, 1924

STODDARD, LOTHROP: *The Rising Tide of Color Against White World Supremacy.* New York, 1920

STOREY, MOORFIELD: *Problems of Today.* Boston, 1920

SUMNER, WILLIAM GRAHAM: *Folkways.* Boston, 1906

TANNENBAUM, FRANK: *Darker Phases of the South.* New York, 1924

THIRTY YEARS OF LYNCHING IN THE UNITED STATES, 1889–1918 (with appendices for years 1919–27). Published by the National Association for the Advancement of Colored People, New York, 1919 (Out of print)

THOMAS, WILLIAM I. (editor): *Source Book for Social Origins.* Boston; 1909 (Fourth edition)

WESLEY, CHARLES H.: *Negro Labor in the United States.* New York, 1927

WHIPPLE, LEON: *Story of Civil Liberty in the United States.* New York, 1927

WOOFTER, T. J., JR.: *The Basis of Racial Adjustment.* Boston, 1925

WOODSON, CARTER G.: *The Negro in Our History.* (Revised edition, first printed, 1923.) Washington, 1928

Files of the *Crisis, Biometrika, The American Journal of Anatomy, Opportunity—A Journal of Negro Life, The Journal of Negro History,* etc., etc.

Pamphlet publications of the National Association for the Advancement of Colored People, the Commission on Interracial Co-operation, American Civil Liberties Union, the Ku Klux Klan, etc., etc.

Those who may wish more extensive references will find excellent bibliographies in *The New Negro,* edited by Alain Locke, and published in 1925; and in Benjamin Brawley's *A Social History of the American Negro.* Monroe N. Work's *A Bibliography of the Negro in Africa and America* (1928) is especially recommended as the most comprehensive source yet published, though it has, unfortunately, like *The New Negro,* some errors of omission and of compilation.

INDEX

i

A NOTE ON THE TYPE
IN WHICH THIS BOOK IS SET

*This book is composed on the Linotype in Bodoni,
so-called after its designer, Giambattista Bodoni
(1740–1813) a celebrated Italian scholar and
printer. Bodoni planned his type especially for use
on the more smoothly finished papers that came
into vogue late in the eighteenth century and drew
his letters with a mechanical regularity that is readily apparent on comparison with the less formal old
style. Other characteristics that will be noted are
the square serifs without fillet and the marked contrast between the light and heavy strokes.*

SET UP,
ELECTROTYPED, PRINTED AND BOUND
BY VAIL-BALLOU PRESS, INC.,
BINGHAMTON, N. Y.
PAPER MANUFACTURED BY
S. D. WARREN CO.,
BOSTON

www.ingramcontent.com/pod-product-compliance
Lightning Source LLC
Chambersburg PA
CBHW071838270326
41929CB00013B/2029